Step Awayyy from the Porcelain!!!!

Step Awayyy from the Porcelain!!!!

A Funny Thing Happened on the Way to Building A Business Empire

Teddy The Tax Man™

Gold Bar Publishing House, Inc.
Hunt Valley, Maryland

Step Awayyy from the Porcelain!!!!
A Funny Thing Happened on the Way to Building a Business Empire

Published by Gold Bar Publishing House, Inc.
Hunt Valley, Maryland

The name "Playboy" appearing in the cover photo and in this book is a registered trademark of Playboy Enterprises International, Inc.

ISBN: 978-1-7328250-0-0 (paperback)
ISBN: 978-1-7328250-1-7 (e-book)

Library of Congress Control Number: 2018912201

First Gold Bar Publishing House, Inc printing: November 2018

Table of Contents

Teddy, Set, Go!

hear many business owners say, "When I was a child, I knew that I'd grow up and have my own business." Well, I can't tell you that. I really don't recall telling my parents that I want to be an Enrolled Agent (a tax professional who is licensed by the U.S. Treasury), a life insurance agent, a retirements rollover professional, an investment advisor, and among the tax virtuosi of the United States, all at the same time. A 1040 laureate. When I look back at my youth, however, it's not hard to believe that I did end up in be-your-own-boss world. At the age of thirteen, I sold seeds. At fifteen, I sold magazines door-to-door. I was very good at both. I won a hatchet for selling seeds. Yes, a hatchet . . . a thirteen-year-old boy with a hatchet . . . a thirteen-year-old *CITY* boy, with a hatchet. And I earned a promotion while selling magazines. But it's amazing how two run-ins with dogs on the same Saturday can change one's mind about a door-to-door job. Anyway, after looking back, should I be surprised that I ended up in the realm of the self-employed? Absolutely not!

> "When I look back at my youth . . . it's not hard to believe that I did end up in be-your-own-boss world."

It all started in August 1978, albeit, not on a good note. Early one Sunday morning, just three months after graduating from high school, I found myself being hoisted from my bed and carried down the steps by my father and two of my brothers. I recall going in and out of consciousness and getting glimpses of people and things as I was being moved along. They rushed me to the world-famous Johns Hopkins Hospital. And yes, there is an 's' at the end of John. (Why any parent would do such a thing to a child, I'll never know.) Anyway, after a whole day of tests, the doctors gave me the dire news. Acute sinusitis! Not just sinusitis. Acute sinusitis! Now, I had never even had even a hint of a problem with my sinuses, so I knew that this was special. My doctor described the problem to me. "Teeodor, you hab a sebere block-ach ob your sinuses. On Tuesday, what we hap to do ees make an enceesion right at your eye brow and eensert a leetle pipe dat will be steecking out ob your head about 3 qvarters of an eench." Wow! Alright. Whatever the doctor says.

Tuesday afternoon after the surgery, I had been returned from the recovery room to my own private room. (I'll bet you haven't used that term in years). I got myself together, struggled over to the mirror and removed the patch that was covering this newly grown horn of mine. It was just like the doctor said. I stared and stared. I wondered what would happen if I just snatched the pipe out. Would I bleed to death? After about eight minutes, I had to get over the fact that I was gazing at a human unicorn. But I had to get over it, so I convinced myself that I was the best-looking mythical creature on that entire floor. The doctor was on his way up to my room to do the test that would show that the sinuses were all clear and I'd be going home in a day or two.

"Okay, Teeodor. Now, I hap to eenject dees saline solution into de pipe and you should feel it drain down your maxillary sinuses and dat will prove da operation successpul. Here goes." He stuck the needle into the pipe extending from my forehead and injected the saline solution. "Do you feel eenything?"

"No."

"Hmmm. Okay, I weel try again." He repeats the process. "Anything?"

"No."

"Okay. Once more. Here goes. Anything?"

"No, Doctor. I don't feel anything draining down my sinuses."

"Hmmmm. I'll be back, Teeodor."

Man! I figured he must be going to get a bigger hypodermic needle than the one he was using. Although, if there was a bigger one, it had to be in the book of world records. I waited and waited and no doctor. I figured he must've gone to lunch. A few long hours later, he sauntered in, with nothing in his hands. He pulled up a chair and began to speak.

"Teeodor, de operation was not successpul. De bone ober your eye is inpected. On Tuesday, we hap to do a much more complicated operation. We hap to make an eenceesion (he's using his right pointing finger and dragging it from the top of his left ear, across the top of his own head to the top of his right ear to demonstrate) from the top of your left ear, all the way across the top of your head, to the top of your right ear. "Den we plip (flip) your skin back and pop out your eyes. Den we will remoob de bone, make an eenceesion in your stomach, remove some pat (fat) and replace de bone with de pat. Okay?" He patted me on my leg, got up and walked out into the hospitally smelling halls and disappeared. He acted as if he had just described to me how to put on brown dress socks on a Sunday morning.

Oh, I know! We're on that hidden camera show, right? We must be. Otherwise, where was his bedside manner? His empathy? Oh yeah. The camera is behind that mirror, right? No, that would be too obvious. Ahaaaa! It was in the doctor's stethoscope! How ingenious! Alright, camera staff and production crew. It's time to jump out and tell me to smile! I'm waiting! I'm waaaiting! (Sigh). There was no camera crew. No camera. And definitely no smile! There were only five of us in that room: my parents, me and the two tears slowly running down my face. Where was my life headed? What was I going to do? Well, I only had one full day before the operation to pull myself together, so I had to convince myself that this was for the best.

Early Thursday morning, they wheeled me to the operating room, where I could see Dr. Bedside Manner patiently (pun definitely intended) awaiting my arrival.

"Teodor, are you ready? We are now going to gib you de anesthesia." They administered the anesthesia. As I was fading into oblivion, he said, "We will hap to cut your hair in order to perform de operation."

"Doctor, will it grow back?" I asked tearfully.

"Yes Teodor. It will."

Liar!! Then how come thirty years later as I'm walking across the parking lot of a west Baltimore pharmacy, a little six-year-old girl (whom I've never seen before) walking with her father is asking me why I have a scar across my head?

In my room, hours after the big operation, Dr. Bedside reviewed. After physically inspecting his work for close to half an hour, he gave his conclusions.

"Teodor, de operation was a success. You will need to stay here a pew days so dat we can monitor you. Ip you want someting to eat later today, you can hab some soup, but nothing solid yet. I'll be back tomorrow. In de meantime, try not to sneeze, because you could blow your brains out, okay? I'll see you to-morrow."

What would this world be without warm and fuzzy doctors? And this time, he even cheated me out of my pat on the leg. I'll address the significance of this whole episode for business own-ers and wannabe business owners a little later on. It's amazing how much of your life's everyday experiences can and will help you when you own a business. You'll see what I'm talking about as you read on.

Believe it or not, within three months, November 1978, I had my first job. I be-came a lifeguard at the Central YMCA in downtown Balti-more. I loved it so much that I recommended one of my high school classmates, Antoine, for the second shift lifeguard position and he was hired in less than two weeks. He also

> **"It's amazing how much of your life's everyday experiences can and will help you when you own a business."**

loved the job! Think about it. He and I were both athletes, and we, each day on our break, could swim, play basketball or take part in any other sport or exercise that the 'Y' offered. We were in our element. All good things must come to an end though. They just don't have to end the way Antoine's did. One day our super-visor called a meeting. We weren't a large staff, so it was easy to tell that Antoine was not at the meeting when it began. The boss didn't beat around the bush.

"I've called this meeting to let you know that Antoine is no longer an employee at the YMCA."

It didn't take a Mensa member to tell that congratulations were not in order. It was something about the boss' eyebrows pointing floorward and the stern tone of voice that told me the reason that Antoine was gone was not a good one. He proceeded. "If he shows up, he is not to be let in for any reason, at any time!" I had a feeling that at least one or two others of the staff knew what happened, but no one said anything to me. I wanted to send Antoine a text message, but it was 1978 and text messaging wasn't even invented until about twenty-six years later and that would've been too long for me to wait to get to the bottom of things. I wasn't able to catch up with Antoine that evening, but when I came in the next day, the front desk clerk enlightened me. Boy, did he enlighten me!

Almost as soon as I crossed the threshold, he said, "You know what happened to Antoine, right?"

"No. All I know is he must've been fired."

"Yep. He sure was."

"Why? What happened?"

The clerk said, "Get this. On his break, he closed the pool, went in the pool area with a buddy of his and locked the door."

"So? What's wrong with—"

"Wait, Teddy! I'm not finished! The two of them got caught smoking reefer in the back of the pool room!"

Okay, reader. Here is your first big decision. If you were an employer, what would you do to or about that person who referred the Woodstock-at-the-Y guy for that position? Would he be forever in the doghouse? Would he get fired too? Would you keep a close watch on him (because birds of a feather flock together)? This is just one of many possible issues that you'll have to deal with as an employer. Are you sure you want to be a business owner?

"Are you sure you want to be a business owner?"

A month after I got the job at the 'Y', December 1978, my cousin recommended me to a store manager to be a part-time shoe salesman. I was able to keep my job as a lifeguard during the week and do the shoe sales thing on weekends and evenings. I wasn't in debt. I wasn't short of money. I think I remember saying, "Hey, I could save all of my money from my second job and some of my money from my full-time job and keep myself in good financial shape." I was good at selling shoes, I was good at saving money, and things were going great. One day, I was speaking to a much older gentleman who had been an employee of the shoe store for quite some time. We were the only two in the store at the moment. I'm not sure how we got on the conversation, but I was expressing to him how shocked I was that one of my eighteen-year-old class-mates was caught having sex with a thirteen-year-old little girl. His matter-of-fact response was, "Shucks. I do that!" Instantly, I thought, "Am I the only one feeling uncomfortable here?" I was only a lowly eighteen year-old employee . . . part-time, no less. But can you imagine being the owner and being trusted with in-formation that could put someone whom you oversee away for good? Or should I say potentially put someone away? Because you know what they say: innocent until proven a creep.

About two years later, and in the same year that I took a data processing course, I took an income tax course. Now, I won't tell you where I studied the course, but it was one of the big-gest tax preparation companies on the "block." They taught me well. Upon completion of the course, I was immediately hired at Montgomery Ward's Tax Service, and lasted there one week before being fired. Yep. My supervisor said that I just couldn't handle the job. Here's what Montgomery Ward's Tax Service wanted out of me: A) To open the office; B) To prepare tax re-turns; C) To be the sole person in the office on my shift; D) To accept cash and check payments for the services; E) To operate the cash register; F) To accept credit card payments using the credit card machine; G) To close the office and a few other tasks, most of which I had never done before. It probably didn't help that when I prepared Mr. Loudermilk's tax return—I'll never for-get that name—I made some very bad copies of his information and gave it all back to him that way. He probably was an insider, or what companies call a mystery shopper, but whoever he was, I know that I didn't do a good job. Plus, they wanted me to do all of this without supervision. But what brand new employee ever wants to say, "No, I don't think I can do what you're asking me to do"? Okay, current and future business owners, this should be an easy one. Be careful not to set your employees up for failure. A new person on the job will say yes to just about anything he/she is asked to do for fear that he/she may soon not be a new employee any longer. Sure. I know what the resumé said.

> " Be careful not to set your employees up for failure. "

So be patient. I'll open your eyes to some things a few pages later. Side note: Where is Montgomery Ward's Tax Service now? I really want to say "Naaaaa naa na naa naaaaaa," right now, but I don't know how to spell it.

I wasn't lazy when I was young. No, I didn't walk barefooted in the snow ten miles to school, while carrying my baby brother on my shoulders after getting up at four in the morning to feed the cows or anything, but I certainly wasn't lazy. I just never felt like cleaning my room or raking leaves or sweeping up or taking out the trash or washing dishes or vacuuming. After taking the income tax course and being jilted by the now long-defunct Montgomery Ward's Tax Service, I began preparing taxes "on the side." A short while after that, in 1979, I got a job as a mail clerk at Alex Brown Investment Bankers, and left the Y. I had even more fun as a mail clerk than I did as a lifeguard. Plus, I was making $135/week, $10 more per week than I made at the YMCA. It paled in comparison to the $5,000 minimum per month that their stockbrokers were making, but I didn't care. My data processing course paid off about six months later. I landed a computer operator job at the Savings Bank of Baltimore in downtown Baltimore, Maryland. Finally! I was into my career. It was 1980. I operated an IBM 360 series computer. Not a puny little do-nothing desktop. Not a teeny-weenie, itsy bitsy chump little sissy laptop. It was gargantuan! A real man's computer! It was the length of about four station wagons, and it was about six feet high. A guy could take a pretty good nap behind one of those babies as long as he wiped the gook out of his eyes before the supervisor returned from the Monday meeting.

Anyway, at this point, I was preparing taxes, I was into my career as a computer operator and I was studying for something else all at the same time. I never thought about it then, but man oh man, how all that juggling helped me when I opened my office outside of the home eleven years later (1991)! That's right! Eleven years later. You see, for the first eleven years in tax preparation, I made house calls. I worked my job at the bank, came home to prepare taxes, and delivered the returns directly to my clients. I met some great people, and I met them in their homes. Take Rosetta, for instance. She had become a client through a referral. Let me paint the picture. She was a sweet young lady of about thirty-one years of age. She was petite, single, with two small children, making good income as a forklift operator, which in itself was interesting considering her size. Each year, I was able to get Rosetta about four thousand dollars in refunds. She was very happy about that and used the money wisely. Each succeeding year, she showed me the upgrades in and around the house for which the previous year's refunds were used. One year, the living room; the next year, the bedroom; the next year, the kitchen. I let her know that I was very proud of how she handled her funds. One day, we were sitting in her living room at the coffee table, winding up the appointment, and I told her, "Okay, you should receive your federal refund in approximately four weeks, and your state refund in about two weeks."

"Okay, Teddy. That's fine with me. It gives me plenty of time to do what I'd like to do."

"Great, Rosetta. By the way, when are you and Booker getting married?"

"Well, we're thinking about next year."

"Oh. Congratulations! I know that you can't wait! Oh, and by the way, don't expect these large refunds once you get married. I won't be surprised if you end up getting about half of what you've been receiving over the last few years."

Rosetta exploded, slamming her right hand against the coffee table and jumping straight up as if hitting the table had propelled her up into the air.

"What? You mean I'm not going to be getting my refunds? That's not fair! They're going to take my money? Oh no! I'm not getting married! No way! The government is always doing something crazy! I will not let them take my money! I am just not going to get married! And that's it!"

I left her house stunned, hair singed, pants creaseless from the explosion. I had not prepared myself for that reaction. I mean, I had no idea that I should've even prepared myself for any particular reaction. Later as I got deeper in my tax practice, I remembered that episode and it taught me that there is absolutely no way that a business owner can be prepared for everything.

> " **there is absolutely no way that a business owner can be prepared for everything.** "

If you always expect the unexpected, I can assure you that a heart attack is closer than you think. By the way, this incident occurred in the early eighties, and I want you to know that as of May 2018, almost forty years later, Rosetta still was not married. Imagine that!

My job in computer operations at the bank was a rewarding one. But in the late eighties, the second banking institution where I was employed ran into trouble. It was the period of the savings and loan debacle that crippled the nation. All the employees got scared. I mean the I-don't-know-if-I'll-have-a-job-tomorrow scared. I was always a positive person. My parents' genes saw to that. I don't believe that a person can be taught to be positive. It's innate. It was passed on from them to me and my siblings. I was confident that some much larger entity would come and be our hero, scoop us up and drive us back into prosperity. I remained confident, unlike all those employees who, prior to the S&L crisis, claimed that they just could not stand working at that place, and were now regretting ever thinking such a thing. Well, it didn't work out. All our potential suitors disappeared faster than money in a spendaholic's (where are George Merriam and Noah Webster when you need them?) checking account. One of those TV shopping networks—POOF! A large well-known agency—disappeared. The mysterious guy from "Joisey" with the heavy mobster-like voice—gone like a shot. On Wednesday of that week, the announcement was made that our doors would soon be closing. I was mad. I didn't even think about my next move at that time; I was too heated. I had put almost ten years of my life into this institution, and due to no fault of my own, or worse, the mismanagement of management, I had to start my life all over? The resumé-writing thing? The classified ads thing? The interviews? The how-to-get-a-job-without-begging-some-person-who-thinks-he/she-has-all-power-in-his/her-hands thing? Fury will make a person's normal, abnormal. I called in s(L)ick the next day. I was longer concerned about my perfect attendance at a job that I absolutely loved. I thought, *I'll just stay home and for the first*

time in my life, be able to kick back and watch the beginning of the
NCAA Basketball Championships, game by game. All of 'em!

What a great weekend that turned out to be! By the time
Monday was knocking on my door, I was thinking to myself:
Wow. I don't even know who should be the target of the harshly-
worded diatribes that went on just five days earlier. Should it be the
folks at the top who will be (financially) well taken care of, after the
last turn of the doorknob? Should it be middle-management, which
had to have had some insight about this whole crazy, life-changing,
make-you-want-to-hide-your-foot-in-somebody's-rectum type of
disaster? Should I have been the target of my own ire because I had
simply gotten too comfortable? Whomever or whatever the cause
of this whole debacle, I was very upset! But I had to move on, and
move on, I did.

I recall preparing tax returns for $25 when I began my prac-
tice. I wanted the business. I needed the business. I was desperate
to grow my practice at all costs, and I thought that lower fees
would be one of the ways to do it. I was working a full-time job
back then, so offering competitive fees wasn't a priority. Getting
the chance to prove myself was my priority. But I must add a
strong warning: be careful doing this with your business, because
if you put yourself out there like that (i.e. lower fees/prices), more
and more prospective clients will expect that of you. If you're
anything like I am, you'll soon tire of the I'll-do-anything-to-
get-you-in-my-office approach. For instance, one day in 2001,

twenty-one years after preparing my first legal tax return, a gentleman called and said, "Listen. I need my tax return prepared, and this is how we're going to proceed." Now reader, you need to understand that by this time, even though Teddy The Tax Man wasn't quite a household name yet, I wasn't hurting for business at all. Remember, it was twenty-one years later, and business had been very good. The caller, in a very stern voice, proceeded.

> " If you're anything like I am, you'll soon tire of the I'll-do-anything-to-get-you-in-my-office approach. "

"Teddy, I'm going to ask you the fee to come in and have my tax return prepared. If you say the fee, and I don't like it, I'm just going to hang up on you. Do you understand?"

I didn't respond.

"Do you understand?"

I said nothing.

"Teddy, are you there? Did you hear me?"

"Yes, I heard you. You said that if I stated the fee and you didn't like it, you were just going to hang up on me. Right?"

He said, "Right!"

My response was, "I'll tell you what. Let me save you the trouble!" Click.

That's when I knew that I had made it in the business world. I doubt seriously that I would've done anything like that in 1980, 1981, 1982 or any time shortly thereafter. In fact, I'm certain that I wouldn't have. Remember, back then I was trying to build my practice, so I was, for lack of a better term, desperate!

Work 'Til You're Tired . . . and Then Work Some More!

We've all had those days on the job that simply wore us out. I mean, down to the point where we left the building, crawled into the car, and took a nap before driving home. That's pretty much the business owner's modus operandi. So be prepared if you're about to become that entrepreneur that you hear so much about. But sometimes, it doesn't pay to give in to that pattern. I once was wrapping up a client's situation over the phone. She was very long-winded, going on and on, talking about something that had nothing to do with taxes, and I was dozing off slowly but surely. You know how it is when you're falling asleep and you don't even realize it. (Don't pretend you've never done it! I know I'm not alone in this.) I remember her asking, "So how do I pay you the tax preparation fee?" My response, as I was kind of, sort of, waking up in the middle of her long dissertation and coming to my senses, was, "You can pay over the phone with a debit card or a credit card or if there's snow on the ground, you can pay with that." Her momentary silence, followed by "Huh?" pulled me out of my daze. "Ah, um, I mean you can mail me a check." To this day, she has never asked me about this . . . and I hope she never does. Readers, plan to get accustomed to those episodes as a business owner. You and Tired will be very close friends.

I did have an advantage over many of my peers. I forged relationships at the Internal Revenue Service and the Comptroller of Maryland, so I was privy to quite a bit that other tax professionals were not. In fact, a lady at the Comptroller of Maryland related to me the following stomach buster:

One day a gentleman with the slowest, southernest drawl ever known to man, called on behalf of his nephew. First of all, if he had a nephew old enough to work, he had to have lived on this earth for a bit. So, no doubt, he was no spring chicken. He had moved up from Mississippi to inject major energy into his life. The gentleman drawler had questions about an envelope his nephew had received. He called the Comptroller's office and described the document that he pulled out of the envelope. "Ohhh- hhhhhhh. Sir, it sounds like it's a W-2 that your nephew received. Did your nephew work last year?" "Why, yay- yes"—apparently the word "yes" has two syllables in

Mississippi—"he did!" "Oh. Alright sir. Your nephew's employer is required to send that statement at the end of the year, so that he can have his tax return prepared and filed. In fact, any person who worked should have gotten one. That's the law, and it has been the law for as long as I can remember. Okay, sir? Is there anything else I can help you with?" After a long pause, the man said, "There sure is. Where can my nephew cash this W-2?"

Owner vs. Employee

Before you decide that you truly want to have your own business, let me first advise you. There are major differences between being an employee and being the owner.

> " There are major differences between being an employee and being the owner. "

At quitting time, if you are an employee, you can't speed out of the parking lot fast enough. In fact, if you're like some of the state of Maryland Department of Assessment employees, you stop answering the phones and close the doors at fifteen minutes before the official close of business, and none of the bosses says anything to you. But if you're the owner, you'll want to make sure that all the lights are off, the thermostat is at the most energy-saving setting, the voicemail is turned on, the burglar alarm is set, and that the toilet isn't left running, wreaking havoc on your water bill.

When the phone is ringing off the hook, employees think like this: "Gosh, I wish these phones would take a break, because I'm in the middle of finding out what happened on my favorite soap opera, *Generic Hospital*. But to you as business owner, those ringing phones mean potential revenue.

If you are just an employee, and a snowstorm hits during working hours, you're out of there. But if you're the owner, you stay behind to back up files and find a contractor to take care of the office grounds—and by then, the weather has worsened and you're stuck at the office with no way of getting home and no way of getting to the nearest hotel, and you have no food, little water, no change of clothes, none of your medicines and a lot of anxiety while your wife is calling every fifteen daggon minutes giving you the blues about why you waited so late to leave in the first place! Well, that's what I hear anyway.

What Shall You Render?

For many folks, deciding what product or service to offer is not even an issue. They want to do what they have already spent years doing while making someone else rich; or they use what it is that they've always dreamed of doing, or what they've done on the side, and make it "legitimate." Finally, there are those for whom just the idea of running their own businesses *is* the dream. Regardless of the product or service, they just think it's time that THEY give the orders. To those folks, my advice is to be careful. If you don't have an idea about what product or service to offer, you could fall for anything. One thing being touted nowadays is home-based businesses. This is what I say: instead of going out and looking for a home-based business, think about what you want or like or are you good at doing, then bring it into your home. There is a tremendous difference. As a business owner, you're already going to be faced with many uncertainties. Don't invite what could be the biggest uncertainty of all: "Will I really like doing this thing that looked so good when they were promoting it at the convention that I spent $100 to get in?" Instead, think about what you are good at, and think about the logistics of doing it from your home. Only then should you make the decision. It's the way to go if working from home is a major factor in your final analysis.

> **" If you don't have an idea about what product or service to offer, you could fall for anything. "**

Stay True to Yourself

My advice is to stay away from multilevel marketing. Also called network marketing, this way of promoting items for sale and at the same time promoting a chance to run one's own business has been around for a long time. Is it normal for people to come up to you grinning and telling you how much they make on their jobs? No! So you should run for the hills if someone tries to rope you into the newest multilevel marketing scheme. I've witnessed goo gobs of these get-rich-never plans bomb out since 1991. You name it. I've seen or been directly involved in it, and it involves many different types of products, from insurance to personal care to telecommunications, to water filters, to kitchen products, to long distance phone services, to juice sales, air filters, children's learning materials, travel representatives, wellness, legal services, mind-blowingly expensive knives, candles, lingerie, herbals, the one that has been around longer than most of the rest and are doing it the AMerican WAY, and finally, cosmetics—even the pink people and the ones who come "calling" and ringing your doorbell. They all claim to be the next lucky stars. And now there's one that claims that it has an aphrodisiac coffee! Give me a break! . . . or at least a sip of that coffee!

But get this, folks: February 28, 2018, marked the beginning of my thirty-eighth year in tax preparation, and I have never seen anyone in multilevel marketing make any money worth the hype.

" I have never seen anyone in multilevel marketing make any money worth the hype. "

Stated another way, of the over 20,000 returns I prepared by the above date, only one of my multilevel marketing clients took in at least twenty thousand dollars. Only one, and he actually showed a loss on his tax return! In fact, for most of those thirty-seven years, only two other of my multilevel marketer clients had even come close to at least bringing in $5,000 in a single year. I have watched and/or even taken part in multilevel marketing for a long time and it's always been the same. Some of the people at the very top *may* make money. The clueless new recruits at the bottom might stay involved for about six months and then disappear. I've found that those who stay in for a little while longer, end up using the product for themselves for a while, then lose interest in the business side of things altogether. They stop going to the meetings. They stop making the calls. That enthusiasm disappears. Plus, they are branded with the multilevel marketing stigma. When people see them walking down the street, they still say, "Look out! Here comes Multilevel-marketing Marvin and he's gonna try to sell us something!" Their friends, close relatives and associates who gave them that sympathy sale in the beginning (referred to as their "warm market" in multilevel marketing jargon), are hoping that he has had his last round in network marketing and that he will stick with his regular job. Readers, I know what I'm talking about! After all that I've just told you, if you still decide that MLM is the way for you, call me a year later and show me what ya got!

Stay Clean

At the age of twenty, I bought my first car. It was brand new, not used. Nine months before I finished paying it off, I bought my first home. Very few of my friends could afford even a used car at that age. None could afford to buy a house. Afford both? Forget it! I had built up a great credit history that paid off at that time and saved me from absolute disaster later in my practice. I've never been drunk. I've never been high. Never been smashed. Never inebriated. Never out of it, bombed or skunked. I can prove the profound effect that that has had on my life. Imagine taking enough drugs or drinking enough alcohol to lose control and your senses on a regular basis. Let's say a person spends may-be a measly twenty dollars once per week on his/her substance of choice. Chump change, right? But twenty dollars per week is $1040 per year. Still chump change, right? Multiply that amount times twenty years of getting wasted and you've lost, at a *mini-mum*, $20,800. And maybe also your teeth and your health! But in many cases, that amount can be blown (no pun intended— well, maybe it was) in a much shorter time span, depending on the frequency and amount of a person's usage. I had friends who, in the late '70s, could easily spend $30 per week for their mind-fogger of choice. That's when I decided that I could put that much in a savings account each week and have it sit there until I was ready to use it. While they inhaled/injected/drank it, I deposited it. That was the impetus to my nest egg building and a major reason why I had to borrow very little money when the time came for me to expand my practice years later.

Drugs didn't get me in the '60s. I was too young.

They didn't get me in the '70s. I was too athletic.

They didn't get me in the '80s. I was too focused.

They didn't get me in the '90s. I was too fatherly.

Drugs, where is your sting? I didn't think that I could be effective if I found myself dead of drug abuse! (Why is it called drug abuse anyway? It's not the drugs that get hurt.) Anyway, I had way too many friends who didn't think that way, and most perished before they were thirty years of age, as a direct or indirect result of substance abuse. Tony. Dead. Drugs. The other Tony. Dead. Drugs. Anthony. Dead. Drugs. Goldie. Dead. Drugs. Hurley, one of only two on this list who made it to fifty, but, dead. Drugs. Rerun. Dead. Drugs. Pedro. Dead. Drugs. Gerald. Dead. Drugs. Morris. Dead. Drugs. Tavon. Dead. Drugs. Mike. Dead. Drugs. Buggy. Dead. Drugs. The other Buggy. Still alive, but a thief. Vincent. Dead. Drugs. Beano. Dead. Drugs. Giggy. Dead. Drugs. His brother, Mike. Dead. Drugs. Push. Dead. Drugs. Douglas. Dead. Drugs. Gary. Dead. Drugs. Craig. Dead. Drugs. Arkbar. Dead. Drugs. Wilbur. Dead. Drugs.

On the other hand, my friends for whom drugs were not an important part of their lives, one of whom is Gordon Hill, are tremendous assets to society. If you currently dabble or regularly use any kind of substance, ask yourself honestly if it has a hold on you. Even if you don't think so, ask someone who knows you well. If the answer is anything other than no, consider making some changes before going into business for yourself. You won't regret it. And don't think it's too late if you're already a business owner. It's definitely not. Make a change as if your life depends on it—because it does! If you love animals, but were about to be attacked and killed by one, you wouldn't hesitate to defend your life by killing that animal if necessary to save yourself, would you? Well, think of that substance you are using as that animal, and defend yourself by getting rid of it. If you want to have an active and productive life, stop partaking in negative activity. Of course it isn't easy. But you *have* to do it. You *can* do it. Remember, your life depends on it.

> " If you want to have an active and productive life, stop partaking in negative activity. "

Employee Turnover

No employee will care about your business the way you do. That's a fact. Ponder this: It's not the '60s anymore, when people routinely got jobs and kept them until retirement. Nowadays the average person changes jobs more than five times throughout his/her lifetime, and your business will simply be one stop on your employees' storied work history, and often you won't

> " No employee will care about your business the way you do. "

see their departure coming. When that employee leaves, you'll need to spend valuable time and money searching for, hiring, and training a new person who may do the same thing to you as the employee before. And even though it's not that something is "being done to you" when an employee leaves, you certainly will take it personally, especially if yours is a small business, where the loss or absence of one person could have a tremendous impact. When that employee says, "Hey boss, I found a new job," your first thought will be, *Now what am I going to do?* But get accustomed to it, and plan to be in this for the long haul. Be proactive by having a hiring and training process already in place, so that you can minimize the inconvenience. Don't say that Teddy The Tax Man never warned you.

On the opposite side of the spectrum, we all know that one employee who has been on the job so long, that she/he thinks she/he owns the place. (I can hear you chuckling right now, because that person's name just popped into your head.) Don't allow it in your business! I applaud the university president who finally had the guts to remove that long-time college basketball coach in Indiana, in the year 2000, after he had been at the college for years. That university president is my choice for person of the ~~year decade century~~ millennium! For years, the coach mauled, slapped, cursed, grabbed, punched and publicly humiliated players whom he thought didn't execute a play properly. As time went on, he got worse. Well, why wouldn't he? Nobody ever stood up to him! A very similar pattern showed in a former mayor of Baltimore, William Donald Schaefer. He said anything he wanted, did anything he wanted to anybody he wanted and nobody would stop him. While he was mayor, if I recall correctly, he went over to a citizen's house and harassed her after the citizen questioned his effectiveness. Another time, in front of the cameras, he explained to some city employees the reason why they were not going to receive raises. When one citizen asked the mayor about his own salary, his response, in front of the camera, was, "I work hard for my job!" What? Are you kidding me?

No Room for Weakness

In 1984, just after the tax rush, I went to Gage, my favorite Baltimore haberdashery. Amongst all that I purchased was a pair of nice long, brown dress socks. They clearly had "Playboy" stitched and prominently displayed on them, along with small bunny ears hanging on them. No kidding, I liked them just because I liked them, having nothing to do with who made them. I wore them over the years as much as any other pair of socks that I had in my rotation, maybe two or three times each month. And they were of good quality. In 2011, twenty-seven years and many 'wears' later, on a Sunday morning as I was about to get dressed for church,

I reached into my drawer, pulled out those socks to wear with my brownish suit, held them up in the air and stared at them for several seconds. Then I burst out laughing. "It hit me like a ton of bricks (or like one of my old girlfriend's biscuits)! The pockets on these Playboy socks weren't for nickels and dimes! Okay, so I can be naïve! I admit it. But you can't afford to be naïve in your business. Some employees, vendors, and clients will sense that and take advantage of you. They may want your product or service, but they want to get it as cheaply as they can get it. If you aren't aware, you will be abused. I don't think I've ever paid a reduced price for anything. Nope. Never! Unfortunately, I'm not bragging. I am the world's worst negotiator. Negotiating is truly one of my weaknesses. I remember going to a car dealership once in search of a new ride. I searched the lot for just short of 1 ½ hours, before finally seeing the vehicle that I just had to have. The salesman and I went in to his desk and he told me that the car was $28,000 and some change. I blurted out, "$30,000 and that's my final offer!" I've never seen a salesperson shake hands and do paperwork so fast. I just abhor having to negotiate. But who says a business owner has to

> " **you can't afford to be naïve in your business. Some employees, vendors, and clients will sense that and take advantage of you.** "

excel at everything? If you've got employees, and you know that you are weak in a certain area, make that a part of someone's job description, especially if it is a regular and ongoing part of your business. But I found out that even your greatest skill will fail you once in a while. Years ago when I was working at the bank, I went out on a much anticipated date with a young lady who also worked there. I had met her the week before. It was fun. It was needed. It was timely, because of some tumultuous times at the job, and in my personal life. Days later, one of my co-workers sent me an electronic message (later called email) asking me how the date went. I used words such as great, fantastic, memorable and awesome. I'm an exceptional speller, but it's amazing how one slip of the stupid keyboard can change the whole story. My response was lengthy, and I closed the story meaning to say, "I got a serious lesson out of it." Somehow or another, an "s" became an "I" and the sentence read, "I got a serious lesion out of it!" My co-worker, ever the confidante, showed it to everyone in his department. After that, I didn't have a lot of young ladies from the bank dialing my number to go out with me. One of my best talents had failed me. It'll happen to you too! Recover, move on and let that be a lesion, uh, I mean, lesson, to you.

Just Ask The Employee

Many a business owner has faced the changing status of his/her business. Whether it's a decline in sales, an increase in expenses a change in trends or an endless line of worker's leaving, there is at least one possible way to hone in on the issue and possibly create a solution: ASK THE EMPLOYEE(S)!

I'm not saying that you always get answers that you expect, when you survey your employees. Like when I was teaching Bible study to my all-time favorite 13 to 18-year-old boys one evening. I was definitely caught off guard. I was trying to make a point that no matter what, we should love a person not solely based on looks. Rather, love a person based on his or her many, many attributes. "As a matter of fact," I said to one student, "Suppose you married the most beautiful girl in the neighborhood. She had a beautiful shape. All the fellows wanted her to be theirs. One day, she got into a horrible accident that disfigured her face. What would you do during your intimate moments together?" He looked up to me after what seemed a sorrowful seven seconds of thought and said, "I'd put a bag over her head!" Now reader, I assure you, I did not see that coming! I mean, how was I supposed to know? That is part of the point here. When you inquire of your employees, you probably will get something other than answers that you would deem useful, but once you sort through all of that, you're bound to get some useful tidbits that could help you to avoid or curtail some troubling times or issues.

Back in the early nineties, a local comedian called and asked if I could help him with his tax troubles. He hadn't filed in a few years and really needed to catch up. Gladly, I took on his case. I told him that he'd better come in before the Internal Revenue

Service showed him firsthand how they had touched Redd Foxx's funny bone. I worked on his situation for about two weeks. We probably talked three or four times over those next few days. Things were going smoothly. I completed one year's return. Then I completed another year's return. I started to feel comfortable with our relationship over that half-month time span. I started feeling so comfortable, that I called one day to give him an update. It was MY time to show him funny. He was away

> " you probably will get something other than answers that you would deem useful, but . . . you're bound to get some useful tidbits that could help you to avoid or curtail some troubling times or issues. "

from his phone when I called, and the caller identification system had not been invented yet, so I left him this message, "This is the IRS. We're coming after you if you don't file all your returns and file them now!" Then I finished the message with a chuckle. "I'm just kidding. This is Teddy The Tax Man. Call me when you get a chance." Apparently, Sir Laffalot couldn't take a joke. He never returned my call! And he never came back! Oh, but you can joke on everybody else, huh Mr. Funny Feelgood?

I'm certain that nowadays, what I did to Chuckles the Cheesehead would be considered wrong on many different levels. But how many times does a business owner go overboard when relating to clients/patients/customers? How many illicit relationships will you get into? Why did you charge one price to the lady who looked like Halle Berry, and another price to Hillbilly Helen? What do you really want from the gentleman whose pecs have peaked? According to some theories (well, mainly mine) 94% of the time, those relationships blow up in public. The other 6% of the time, you will worry that they will. So consider reconsidering when she walks in with a wiggle or he swaggers in the door almost gliding across the floor. Think long term. Think relationship, as in patron.

Ms. Sue was in her early sixties and single. She had no one to whom she was required to answer. The only other occupants of the house were her two cats. She was outwardly upbeat, but five decades of life had made her pretty cynical. I helped her with her retirement plan and caught her up with all her tax returns. I could tell that the things that bothered most folks didn't bother her much. She'd seen it all. She'd heard it all. She'd been there. She'd done that. She got the T-shirt. . . . with her name emblazoned on it! . . . in red! She was supposed to come in one Saturday morning so that I could roll her 401(k) over to an IRA. This was a very important appointment. After the tax season, I rarely set appointments for Saturday, especially if only one client was supposed to come in that day. This was mainly because if I went to the trouble of changing my schedule at home on a day when I could be with the family, and that one person didn't show up, I'd be pretty hot! The temperature gets turned up even more when Mr. or Mrs. Absolutely-must-see-Teddy The Tax Man-on-a-Saturday is so thoughtless that I don't even receive a call explaining why the chair across from my desk will be missing buttocks today! Anyway, when I got to the office that bright beautiful Saturday morning, my phone light was blinking, showing that I had one voicemail message. All I could think was, *Oh no! It had better not be . . . !* I calmed down enough to check the message. "Hi Teddy. It's me, Sue." *Here it comes. Get ready, Teddy.* "I won't be able to make it today." If I were the profane type, a-cursing I would go, right at this point. I would just let 'em rip. Right there, right then, as soon as I heard, "It's me." *Dag it! I could've stayed in bed an extra 8 hours. Instead, I wake up and travel 26 miles for this?* The voicemail continued. "Unfortunately Teddy, my house was broken into last night while I was asleep." (Sigh) *And I'm the one complaining that she didn't come in? (Sigh again.)* "The police are here taking my report and I have no idea how long they'll be." Man! I could've swallowed my tongue. I called her to find out if there was anything that I could do.

"Well, since the forms are already done and just need my signature, can you just bring them by? And I'll give you those prior year returns that you wanted to look at."

"Okay, Ms. Sue! I'll be there in half an hour."

I gathered the paperwork and took off to her house. The guilt pushed me down the road and got me to her house in about 12 minutes. The police had finished their report and had left. I walked in the house and since I've got great nose vision, I could tell that the 2 cats weren't afar off. I could ALSO see the evidence of some knucklehead's thoughtless damage and just felt probably almost as helpless as she. I didn't want to stay too long, yet I wanted to be there to show her that compassion was not passé, and that she shouldn't give up on society. She thanked me and appreciated my going the extra mile under the circumstances. As she handed me the retirement paperwork, I began to walk toward the door. "Oh, I almost forgot." She reached down in the corner and grabbed the bag that had the previous years' tax returns in it. "Here are the tax returns." As she was handing me the plastic bag, she said, "And be careful. My cat did his business on that bag."

What's in a Business Name?

When I was a little boy, my two older brothers had a nickname for me. They teased me by calling me Foot-long. Why? They said that I had a head that was the size and shape of a foot-long hot dog. Believe me: I do not have a foot-long shaped head. I really don't! And when you see me, let me know if you agree. But apparently, they thought the name fit. They thought that name painted a picture, and that if they used my nickname to a person who didn't know me, that person would be able to pick me out of a lineup using the side view. Here's a lesson for all of you future business owners: When starting your business, let the name of the business paint a picture. Can you tell me what product/services these businesses offer?

Carter, Inc vs. Carter Medical Supplies, Inc
Shawty's Shop vs. Shawty's Shoe Shop

If the trucks from each of those businesses were going down the street, only two of them would be memorable and potentially interest onlookers. This may seem so obvious now that I've pointed it out, but the next time you're

> "When starting your business, let the name of the business paint a picture."

out on the road, in the mall, or just walking down the street, count the number of times you see a business whose name doesn't give any indication as to what product or service it offers. After all, if you hand a person your business card, and the person needs to ask what you do, what's the purpose of the business card?

Is naming your business that simple? No. There's a lot more involved than just deciding, "My business shall be called Merciful Mercenaries, LLC." After you've decided what product or service you'll offer, you, your tax advisor, attorney or whomever else you'll be using to set up your business will check with your state to see if the name that you have chosen has already been taken by someone else. I'll tell you right now, that there is a good possibility that it has been, so don't be disheartened. In fact, that's why I recommend having more than one possible name for your business, until it's completely set up. It will amaze you how many other entrepreneurs had the same idea and name for their businesses, as you, and the bigger your state, the higher the chance that the name of your entity has been already taken, even if you've never heard that name publicly. **Very important: Don't be fooled into thinking that no other company can have the same name as yours.** It surely can. But no other company in your state can be *registered* the same as yours. There's a difference: If I wake up one afternoon (I'd love to sleep late one day, but I'm a business owner) and decided that my company will be called Sweetie's Pies, I could just hang my sign, bake my pies and begin. I could sell to my heart's content. West side. East side. South Side. North Side. I could put a hurtin' on the community's cholesterol. I could do all that without registering with the state, but it wouldn't be a smart move.

First, if I handled it that way, I could only be a sole proprietorship (a business that can only be owned by one person and offers no protection of the owner's personal assets), which might not be the best entity type for my business. Why? Because in order for your business to be just about any other entity other than a sole proprietorship, such as an S-corporation, C-corporation or LLC (all of which I will discuss later), it absolutely must start by going through your state or whichever state in which you decide to register.

Second, if a business has already correctly registered with the state and you end up naming your business the same, that business could take legal action against you and the entity that you struggled

> " Don't be fooled into thinking that no other company can have the same name as yours. "

so hard to open and maintain. Then, what would happen to your way of earning a living? You could go broke simply because you didn't take one day to register your business properly (because despite what anyone tells you, in many instances, it only takes one day). So, please do not create business cards, buy domain names, set up websites or engage in any other form of advertising before registering your business with the state.

Apropos of nothing. Again. I can't name anyone who ever regretted NOT taking illegal drugs!

When naming your business, you can try to generate interest by giving it a really interesting name. Funny and interesting is my personal preference. Here are a few names that you can consider, based on your product or service. I give you license to use them:

A) Lawn mowing—I'm Gonna Kick Your Grass

B) Passenger pick-up service—Driving Miss Crazy

C) Rings and necklaces—The Judge & The Jewelry Too

D) Medicinal marijuana—High Hopes

E) Your neighborhood tavern—I'll Drink to That

F) Optometry—I'll Blink to That

G) An ice skating establishment—I'll Rink to That

H) A weight loss center—I'll Shrink to That

I) Your local MENSA chapter—I'll Think to That

J) A paleontologist—I'll Link to That

K) A furrier—I'll Mink to That

L) A diaper service—I'll Stink to That

In the beginning, I was willing to do *anything* to get a new client. I recall having to use the men's room very badly one day. The phone rang again after I had just spent a half hour trying to convince another caller that I should be his tax professional. I had already been "holding it" for longer than any person on this earth ever held. Come to think of it, I had probably broken the record for such an event. But there was no way that I'd miss out on an opportunity to reel in a new client. After all, it was one of my first years after transitioning from a full-time employee in corporate America where my check came like clockwork every other Friday, to a solo career where I'd better convince every caller to come in or I might one day go home to see a sign on my lawn that I didn't put there. "This is Teddy The Tax Man speaking. May I help you?" Wouldn't you know it? The caller didn't ask for directions to my office or another question that could be answered quickly. Nooooo! He asked probably every question that a new caller could ask. It seemed as though he asked me to recite every word in the entire Internal Revenue Code, and follow it up with the Gettysburg Address. I remember him asking about interest deductions. I was in agony. "Well, you can't deduct awwllll of your credit card interest, but you can deduct mortgage interest on your hooome." The pains kept coming harder and sharper and there was only one way to relieve them. All I could envision was what my relief would feel like. Reader, are you wondering why I didn't just get the caller's phone number and call back? Well, I needed to make every potential client an actual client. The mortgage had to be paid. There was no way that I was going to chance losing an opportunity to make some money. I didn't want to show any sign of uncertainty, instability or disinterest. It's the quickest way to lose that uncertain potential client. Finally, after what seemed another eternity, the phone conversation ended. I remember throwing the phone on the hook and running/waddling the only way a person in that situation could, away from the desk and in the direction of relief. Ten more feet to go! Five and a half feet . . . Pure porcelain in my purview! Two feet . . . Aw crap (no pun intended)! Too late! (Sigh) Well, I'd better have MJ send me a new pair that will make me "feel good all under." How embarrassing! Oh! Wait a minute! Why be embarrassed? No one will ever know. The client did make an appointment to come in, so although my large intestine and colon may have suffered, I won this battle. I think. We'll see in a few years.

I'd love to tell you, the aspiring business owner, to make up your mind beforehand how far you'll go to earn that dollar. The truth is, there is no way for me to say it. I'd love to say that some limits are obvious, but that's not real life and they don't apply to every business owner in every situation.

Here's one thing that you should remember: If you give an unadvertised discount to a client, patient or customer, that's not the end of it. The client will tell others, despite the fact that you asked to keep it between just the two of you. The next thing you know, your budget is shot and you'll find that you may as well have not given the discount in the first place. There is a certain amount that you must make off of each sale, and if you don't, your business will go the way of the dodo bird. That's a hard fate to suffer after years of dreams and planning for a successful business.

> " If you give an unadvertised discount to a client, patient or customer, that's not the end of it. "

S Corporation vs. LLC vs. Sole Proprietorship by Choice

You've painstakingly (or not) decided what product or service you'll offer, and of course it's not multilevel marketing. If you think your problems are over, you have another think coming. You now must decide what entity type your business will be. The possibilities aren't endless, but they are numerous. Can you guess which is best between an S-corporation, a C-corporation, a single-member LLC, a multi-member LLC, a partnership or a sole proprietorship? I'll let you think about it for a moment. (Insert game-show thinking music here). Okay. Time is up! If you said "S-corporation," you are right! If you said "C-corporation," you are right. If you said "LLC," ding, ding, ding! If you said "Sole proprietor," bingo! The truth is that there is no best entity type. Your profession, service or product should be a gigantic factor in your decision-making process when trying to choose an entity type. Unfortunately, nowadays, new business owners are choosing the same entity type that a buddy, colleague or their Uncle Henry the barber chose, without first getting a professional opinion. The popularity level that S-corporations achieved in the '80s will more than likely pale

> " Your profession, service or product should be a gigantic factor in your decision-making process when trying to choose an entity type. "

in comparison to the popularity level that LLCs began to realize in the nineties. Why? One of the reasons is the cost to set an LLC up, but another factor is the relative simplicity of remaining federally and state compliant. For instance, if your entity is an LLC and there are no employees (the owners of the LLC are referred to as members, and for payroll purposes are not considered employees) no payroll reporting is necessary, so the LLC doesn't have to pay a payroll service provider the cost of doing weekly, monthly, quarterly and most annual reports. An S-corporation that doesn't have payroll during a given period still has to pay to have federal and state payroll reports sent in. That's right. Even if there was no payroll, reports still generally must be sent in to the IRS, the state withholding department, and the state unemployment department. It's almost as if the S-corporation, in a sense, is paying for nothing. Furthermore, most S-corporation owners (also called shareholders) who work in the business instead of just owning it—and that's 100% of my S-corporation clients over thirty years—are considered employees, so there will always be payroll reports and fees for those.

The Good, The Bad and the Ugly Employee

Employees can only come from one of two places; heaven or hell. Apparently, it was Mike's turn to be sent up. As a brand new first-time-ever computer room supervisor at the bank, I got my middle-management indoctrination through Mike, a computer operator whom I supervised. Just to remind you, people have always seen this invisible sticker across my forehead that reads N-A-I-V-E. I think it's time that I acquiesce. Why? It's called a retrospec-

> "**Employees can only come from one of two places; heaven or hell.**"

tive self-analysis. You see, Mike was by no means a rookie to the work world. He had been around the meadow a few times (and certainly consumed a few of the plants therein, if you get where I'm coming from). I guess he was late-thirties-ish. A single Vietnam vet, he always had a military story at the ready. And boy, were they some good and entertaining stories. He used terms like Saigon, Tet Offensive, VC and Ho Chi Minh, none of which I knew much about. Man! I just wanted to pull up my chair, get my popcorn, and forget about banking reports. But entertaining wasn't the only word that I could use to describe Mike, not by a long shot. I realized this when one day he headed out for lunch/dinner (we worked 3:00 PM–11:00 PM). He asked me what he could get for me from his favorite sub shop. I jumped right on that offer. Shucks. I'd swim the English Channel with an elephant on my back for a good sub! Two and a half hours later, Mike reappeared. "Man, that sub shop employee must be crazy! He fixed your sandwich and had the wrong stuff on it. I didn't realize it until I got about one block away from here, so I had to turn around and go all the way back to the store and make him change it! Don't you know he gave me fits about correcting the order? I mean we stood there arguing for about twenty minutes!" Well, reader, I'm not quite that naïve. At least the lie was entertaining. But that adventure was small potatoes compared to this next one. I guarantee you that you can't tell a better story than what you are about to read. One day, I noticed him grimacing and seemingly writhing in pain.

"What's wrong, Mike?"

"Uhh. Ooooh. I'm not sure Teddy, but . . . but I think I'm stopped up. You know, constipated."

Please understand by this time there had been many, many Mike-ventures, including his failure to show up at work when he claimed he was still snowed in two weeks after a snowstorm, even though four consecutive days of warm weather after the storm melted most of the snow. I indulged him. I simply had to.

"Oh no, Mike! Are you going to be okay?"

"Oh, I don't know. I think I'll have to leave."

"Oh okay. Go ahead. Take care." The grimacing was one thing. The writhing in pain was another. But at this point, he was walking away and really playing this thing up. Picture this: As he was walking down the hall, he was limping, and his right foot was turned inwards almost as if he had a deformity. To be honest, I didn't know that a simple case of the clog-ups could do that to a person. But it didn't stop there. His car was parked in a parking lot within view of the building, so for the total of a block and a half, he carried on the charade. Limping, humped over, almost like Quasimodo, knowing that I was probably going the extra length to watch him from our second-story hall window. I watched until he disappeared into the car lot under the bridge where he was parked. The next day, he didn't come in. The day after, he didn't show up. The following day, no Mike. Not only did he stay away from work, but he didn't call either. Calls to his home went unanswered. My boss's boss even began to inquire. Just over two weeks later, guess who walked into the computer room? You got it! I sat down with him after the shift change and asked how he was doing, still trying my best not to erupt—sorry for that expression—with laughter in anticipation of what I knew would be a humdinger.

"Oh my goodness, Teddy! I never want to go through anything like that again!"

"What? What do you mean, Mike? What happened?"

"Well, I went from doctor to doctor and none of them could help me out. But I finally went to one who gave me something. I finally went . . . you know! And guess what, Teddy? When it came out, it was twenty-six feet long! It was so bad, that I had to call the plumber to unclog the plumbing in the house!"

Now reader, Mike wasn't six years old. He was in his late thirties. I wasn't five years old. I was in my late twenties. So, I'm not sure which one of us was supposed to believe this massive fable that Aesop would have envied. My question is, "What would YOU have done if you were Mike's boss and he told you that tall tale, uh, fib, uh okay, that grandiose lie from the pit of hell?"

Needless to say, after that, some other employer had to worry about Mike and his unique situations. But wait a minute! Now I wonder if he had ever even been IN the military!

The employee on the opposite end of the heaven-hell spectrum was Marlene. I'd give anything to have an employee like her. She knew her job well and performed it very well. Plus, she was very reliable. Heaven sure missed her when she came down. She probably had one of the best overall attitudes that I've ever seen in an employee anywhere. If the bank would have had a better ending or even a decent continuance, I would have definitely spoken up for her to get her into another position in data processing. I promise you that, wherever she may be working, she's doing well for her employer.

The Things They Don't Tell You

If you attend a conference on starting a business, there will be things that won't be covered that you will still have to learn. That's one of the reasons why I wrote this book. Remember the whole episode with Dr. Bedside? At the time, I was still living at home with my parents, so while I was recuperating, I didn't have to worry about income to pay for a mortgage. I had no bills and life was a whole lot simpler. But imagine being a business owner and being laid up and shut down and out with no way to make money. You may as well flush everything down the same commode that Mike used to rectumfy, I mean rectify his situation. The answer? Make sure you have disability insurance! You'll need coverage so that if you are down and out and unable to earn a living, you will be able to pay the mortgage, buy groceries and take care of electric bills and all those other monthly monsters that don't seem to care that you're not making money at the time. And the younger you are when you start a disability policy, the lesser your cost. Incredibly, during one recent two-year span, I had only sold one of these policies. That's how important the few entrepreneurs who do know a thing or two

> " **Make sure you have disability insurance!** "

about this type of insurance think it is. But I promise you, a disability insurance policy can save you from certain ruin. Want to see your savings account drain quickly? Get injured to the point where you can't work and earn income. You'll only have to learn this lesson once. In fact, you may be only able to experience it once, because once is all it takes.

I witnessed firsthand a situation that could've ended in total disaster, due to a business owner not having a disability policy. I was on an Airline's flight #296 on May 31, 2011, at 8:20 AM, headed to San Diego for my annual retirements conference. The new strategies that I was hoping to learn would be great for my clients wanting to roll over a retirement plan. The day had begun as normal as any of my days that included flying to a conference. You know: I woke up late, got to the airport late, took too long to go through the TSA check-point, and ran to the gate in just enough time to board. You know. Normal. It was a good takeoff. By then, my adrenaline had slowed, my mind started to mellow, and my body just gave in. What a great time to take a nice nap! Off I go into zzzzz land! (I never knew why Z's represent the sounds that a sleeping person makes. It doesn't make sense to me. I've never heard a person buzz while sleeping.) After about 92 minutes in flight, I slowly came out of my sleep to someone shouting, "Is there a doctor on the plane? Is there a doctor on the plane?" All I could think of was, "Oh my goodness, they're asking for a doctor! Somebody's in REAL trouble!" After what seemed a few more minutes, I could hear, "We may have to divert the plane!" Oh my gosh! Divert the plane? Whoooooaaa! What in the world is going on? I recall seeing out of the corner of my eye, my very successful colleague Ron Allison, who was sitting beside me when the plane took off, walking down the aisle, apparently headed towards the restroom. If he's the one who's sick, he sure is handling it well. I mean, if he were to walk any slower, he'd legitimately be considered to be walking in slow motion. Then I noticed that there were people buzzing in the aisle. Some were approximately six feet from me. Reader, you've got to understand, I was coming out of a very nice, deep, deep sleep, so it was taking me a while to shake the cobwebs out of my head and come back to reality. Oh oh! Some people were gathered about 4 feet from me, so I may be able to help the victim without leaving my seat. Why is there so much loud talking? . . . crazy people! A guy can't even have a decent in-flight two-hour period of shut-eye without . . . Wait! Why is this lady whom I don't even know, shouting in my face and holding my hand? Huh? What do you mean am I alright? Leave me alone, and let me catch up on my daggon sleep, you foolish people! You're waking me up out of a nice, restful sleep to ask me am I alright? That doesn't make sense! Well, no, I'm not alright, because YOU'RE WAKING ME UP OUT OF MY DAGGON SLEEP TO ASK ME AM I ALRIGHT! Come to find out, I wasn't alright. Apparently, I had died, thirty-thousand feet in the air. Wow! THAT close to heaven in more ways than one!! The loud talking? The buzzing? The noise? It was an ad hoc team that jumped into action at the time of my dire need. Thank you, lady who was shouting in my face, asking me was I alright. Turns out, she was a nurse. Thank you, man who spent time doing an impromptu on-sight, in-flight examination. Turns out, he was a doctor. After I came to, he told me that he hadn't been able to find a pulse for quite a while, and as much as he was hoping for a positive outcome, it was not evident that that was going to be the actual result. When the plane landed, I was immediately taken to The University of San Diego (I think) where they kept me for about four hours as a precaution. Test after test proved that there was nothing wrong, so off to my conference I went. Now, imagine. If the news had been worse, and/or if I had been left unable to work, financial disaster would've been right there on my doorstep, waiting. Financial disaster is no fun when you provide for a wife, support two children, and love spoiling

> **" If the news had been worse, and/or if I had been left unable to work, financial disaster would've been right there on my doorstep, waiting. "**

three grandchildren. Oh, and by the way, my colleague Ron? He was the first to recognize that I was in deep trouble, and he summoned the flight team, who summoned the medical professionals. I was correct when I thought that I saw Ron walking down the aisle. He was vacating his seat, so that the professionals could get to me, to do what they did. Wow, Ron! You know what? I am so thankful, that I'm going to roll over your 401(k) at a discounted 5% commission!

I asked the airline for the in-flight report that broke down the incident, but they have a strict policy that does not allow the sharing of this type of information. I completely understand. I will compliment them and say though, that they handled it well, and after my brief hospital stay, I did feel 'free to move about the country.' Here is what they wrote to me:

Dear Teddy The Tax Man,

Thank you for contacting us. I appreciate the opportunity you've given me to respond to your concerns.

Please allow me to explain that records relating to in-flight medical emergencies and other irregular operations are maintained internally to protect the interests and privacy of both our airline and our Customers. As such, I'm unable to provide the records you've requested. However, we can understand your desire for information related to your medical situation onboard Flight #296, and we're happy to summarize the information available to us.

Our Flight Attendants recall that you were not feeling well, and shortly after, you became physically ill. They stated that you were not responding to verbal cues, and they worked with another Passenger onboard, who was a physician, to alert the Captain of the situation. When the Captain became aware, an inflight medical consultant was contacted. The Crew administered oxygen to you and continued to monitor your condition throughout the flight until reaching San Diego, where medical personnel met the aircraft at the gate.

We hope you will find this information useful for your purposes. Your patronage is very important to us, and we hope to welcome you onboard another 'free-to-move-about-the-country' flight again soon.

Sincerely,

'Free-to-Move-About-The-Country' Airlines
The file reference number for your email is 2236934602647.

Can you imagine what would have happened to my family and me if that scary episode had resulted in an extended stay in the hospital? No money coming in, yet bills still coming to my inbox. Again, I say, get disability insurance!

Something else you probably won't learn about at a conference are the taxes for your employees. As a business owner, as of May 2018, you are still required to pay half of the total of social security that goes into your employees' social security accounts. Moreover, you are required to pay half of the total Medicare that goes into your employees' Medicare accounts. These mandates could change at any time, but for now, that's the way it is, and business owners really need to plan for these expenses the way they would plan for utility expenses, supply expenses, rent or business mortgage expenses.

Is it better to be embarrassed in front of a client with whom you are familiar, or one who is brand new to your practice/business? Because nothing beats this conundrum: I was on the phone with Narin who wanted me to help her roll over her retirement from a job where she was no longer employed. She had been a client of mine for quite a while, then she got

> " business owners really need to plan for these expenses the way they would plan for utility expenses, supply expenses, rent or business mortgage expenses. "

married and she, her husband and I really looked forward to meeting at least once per year for tax preparation, retirements, or for whatever reason we needed to meet. "Okay, Narin," I said. "We've discussed the rollover. Now, we have to call the company where the funds currently are, so that they can send you the paperwork that needs to be filled out. Just hold on, and I will dial their number. When their phone begins to ring, I'll switch back over so that when they answer, we'll both already be on the line." I called the 800 number. The phone began to ring. I switched back over and quickly said, "Are you still on, Narin?" She replied, "Yes, I'm here." No sooner had she said that, I heard the other phone pick up. This was the greeting, verbatim: "Welcome to America's HOTTEST talk line! Ladies, to talk to exciting and interesting guys free, press 1 now. Guys, hot ladies are waiting to talk to you. Press 2 to connect free now! As I began to tuck my head in my shoulders and melt away, it seemed that by some miracle, Narin never heard any of it!! Of course, I had to ask her to make sure. I just really needed to know. Through her laughter, I could barely hear, "No, I'm certain that I heard NONE of that! Boy, will this give my husband a good chuckle!" That event could have taken a lot of different turns. Fortunately, I was able to retain the color in my face and move on with the rest of my day.

And the Truth Shall . . .

Cheryl was the girlfriend of Al, who was one of my clients. I had never met her face to face. In fact, the only time I ever spoke to her was when I called the home they shared, trying to reach Al. At one point she decided that if I was a good enough tax preparer for Al, I would be good enough for her. She made an appointment and came in one evening. As she walked in my office, she headed towards the chair in front of my desk where each client sits for the appointment. As she went to seat herself, her eyes wandered all over my office. Now, remember, I had never met this young lady. "Teddy, your office is a mess!" I burst out in laughter, because it's the same sentiment I had been hearing for many years from my longtime clients. It's that one thing that they can't wait to talk about when they come in. Forget about taxes! Well, as usual, I got a bit of enjoyment out of the moment and got down to tax preparation. "Your office is a mess!" she repeated. This time I laughed, but not quite as hard as the first time. I continued on with the interview, and after a few more moments, she again lamented, "I'm really serious, Teddy. Your office is very messy! I'm sorry. I'm just a person who likes to tell it like it is!" At this point, I was getting quite bothered. Again, remember, I don't know this lady from a brunette turtle in pumps! On with the interview. "Okay, Cheryl. What's your date of birth?" I asked. "April 15, 1955," She replied. I typed it in. I looked at her. I looked at the computer. I looked at her. "Hmmm," I said. "What, Teddy? Is anything wrong?" Cheryl asked. I said, "You look way older than that!" Her eyes opened four times bigger and her lower chin did everything except hit the floor. Then I said, "You see? The truth hurts sometimes, doesn't it?" I didn't hear a peep out of her for the rest of the appointment.

The situation with Cheryl reminds me of an old adage that says the customer is always right! Phooey! I've never believed that, and when you begin to operate your business, don't fall into that stupidity! What I have realized in these thirty-plus years is that if you allow it, your patrons will take advantage of you. Obviously, every person with whom you transact business doesn't have that mindset, but all it takes is one

> " **if you allow it, your patrons will take advantage of you.** "

to ruin your day. The problem is, how does a business owner prepare for that situation? We certainly can't offer our products and services with a chip on our shoulders, just waiting for that one patron who will ruin the day, because for the most part, we never know who he or she might be. Also, that chip will be evident to each patron you serve and it would be unfair to those who come before the "ruiner." Take for instance, Peter, a skip-tracer. I think they're called bounty hunters nowadays, but this was back in the early nineties. I have to be honest with you. Peter was a pest, and seemed to be just a little "off." His wife was no brain force either. You know exactly what I mean. They seemed to be perfect for each other. It seemed to me that at any moment, two austere and physically fit gentlemen in white coats could come along and escort both of them to the loopy locale. I called their house one day and she answered. Without even knowing who it was (because the caller identifying system had not yet been invented), or why she was being called, she answered, "What! What do you want?" That's how she answered her phone! I took it personally, just like everything else. I just do not have thick skin. My response? I prepared their return, charged them double what I charged the year before, and never saw them again.

Revelations

I don't expect those who never owned a business to understand this, but owning a business will consume you! I think about my business when I'm home, while I'm driving, while I'm on vacation, while I'm on a plane, while I'm at weddings, while I'm in the men's room, while I'm in the ladies' room (but that's another story), while I'm writing this book, while I'm at parties, while I'm in the shower, while watching the game, while I'm in class, during altar call, when I'm at the hospital, while I'm at the gym, while I'm shoveling snow, when I'm at dinner, while I'm changing the baby's diaper (that's

" owning a business will consume you! "

when I think about Mr. Pellgram), while I'm at funerals, while I'm on the court, while I'm in court, on the weekends, on my anniversary. . . . Most of my dreams are dumb and incomplete. But dream time is my only real getaway from the rigors of being a tax professional, investment advisor, insurance representative and employer. And since sleep experts say that many dreams only last for a few seconds, well you should be getting the picture. Once I dreamed that two oranges were chasing me down the street. Just before one could spit out a person on me, I woke up, and remembered that I forgot to call the IRS for a client. Another time, my grandson, who was 1 year and 9 months old, spent the night on Christmas Eve 2009. We woke up Christmas morning (of course, the business on my mind) to the toys and the fun that children should wake up to. At one point, I asked him if he wanted me to read to him. Up on my lap he climbed. I grabbed my favorite eleven-pager and took my time reading it out aloud to him. He loved helping me turn the pages. That's always part of the fun for him. After we finished, he excitedly jumped off my lap as if rejuvenated, and went on to play. My goodness! I never thought he'd enjoy my pamphlet on variable annuities so much! Immediately afterwards, my mind went to wondering if I electronically filed Ms. Stewart's tax return a few months ago. Are you sure you want to be a business owner?

> " **If you are a business owner, the job really is with you all the time, if not physically, then mentally.** "

If you are a business owner, the job really is with you all the time, if not physically, then mentally. When lay people say TGIF, they mean that they're happy that they can prepare to party like it's 1999. When I say TGIF, I'm thinking that after a long, grueling week at the office, I can't wait to come in on the weekend while the phones aren't ringing, to catch up on the work that I did not finish during the last five days.

But, believe me, there is nothing like enjoying the fruits of owning a prosperous business. I've gone to many places and done great things that the average eight-hour-Eddie has never and will never be able to afford to do. I've been all over the continental United States. I sent my wife on a trip to Egypt. I've enjoyed the 'round-the-clock excitement of no fewer than eight cruises. I've flown and splash-landed in a water plane in Vancouver, British Columbia. I almost fell out the boat when I witnessed a blue marlin jump and rip the fishing line in the Cayman Islands. I parasailed in paradise. Twice! Nice! I scuba-dived in Mexico (where I found out that if you're 22 feet deep and bang your knee on hard coral, and you scream, nobody can hear you). I stood on a boat about thirty yards away from a pod of killer whales in Alaska. I did the hula in Hawaii. I glided across the Everglades in an airboat. And I finally had the time of my life on my dream trip that took me across the International Date Line, halfway around the world to beautiful Fiji!

> " believe me, there is nothing like enjoying the fruits of owning a prosperous business. "

Would I do it again? My answer is an emphatic YES. But the next time, I wouldn't spend so much time in the office. (Believe that part, and I'll sell you Mt. Rushmore with Whistler's mother on it.)

Big Ralphie kind of went by his own rules. Early sixties, borderline retiree, tavern owner, 6' 3" and about 267 pounds with blond medium length hair and bad feet. You could not have created a more perfect character for his business. The only thing missing was the cigarette. I'm not sure that he ever smoked, but that was probably good anyway, because it's hard to put a cigarette in your mouth with handcuffs on. You see, his establishment was raided at least three times for illegal gambling. But I didn't care about all that. My issue was a whole lot more personal. Big Ralphie used his right pointing finger to twist and turn into certain orifices of his body while sitting right there in front of me. RIGHT THERE IN FRONT OF ME! I don't know whether he just had no shame about it or if he wasn't aware that he was doing it. The second time that I noticed his finger-spinning ritual,

I knew that I had to do something. After every appointment, I shake hands with the client. That's what we do in America. As the appointment was coming to a close, he stood up and extended his right hand for a shake. Fear just overtook me! I'll tell you now, I've never thought so fast in my entire life. I quickly acted as if I had spilled the envelope sealer glue on my hands. "Uggh!" I raised my hands as high as my chest, with my hands hanging sort of limp, the way a person would if a person really had wet, dripping hands. That way, he would see that I was not in hand-shake mode. And as he was moving toward the door, making his closing comments, I let him see me very slowly walking towards the restroom (to wash off the imaginary glue) still with my face toward him, listening to his every word as I began to increase the distance between the two of us. As I reached the restroom door (I don't know why I'm calling it the restroom; I never got any rest in it as a business owner; hence, STEP AWAYYY FROM THE PORCELAIN!!!!), he uttered his last words—something about a judge, a verdict and bail—and exited the office. I stepped in the bathroom long enough to hear the outside door close, came out and prepared for the next client, without worrying about a con-taminated right hand.

But gangsters aren't the only ones who commit this unclean act. I had a pastor client who, well, let's just say that it wasn't un-clean lips that I was worried about. If I ever ate at his house, it definitely would be my LAST SUPPER!

To Family, or not to Family: That is the Question

Try asking this question to various people you know: If you were an employer, would you hire a sibling? A parent? A cousin? You probably wouldn't be amazed at the high number of "no" answers you'd get. And not just a "no" but an adamant one. I've asked this question throughout both my computer and tax preparation careers, and I can recall very few times getting a "yes" answer. The reason I've heard most is, "My family and I don't get along." I've also heard, "I don't want to be around my family for eight hours at the workplace and the rest of the day at home." And sometimes, I hear "I know too much about my family."

I would like to open your eyes to the possibility that a family member can indeed come to work for you. In October 1994, I was at a crossroads. Two years prior, my sister had worked part-time for me. One year prior, my father had worked part-time for me. But now, I was in that no-man's-land where my practice was too large for just me and a part-timer, but really not large enough for another full-timer other than me. I was starting to panic because in just a few more months, the tax rush would start, and I wouldn't be able to handle it. I didn't have time to post the job announcement anywhere, and I

> " I would like to open your eyes to the possibility that a family member can indeed come to work for you. "

definitely would not have the time to answer the phone calls and read each résumé in addition to taking care of my current clients. So, I got the bright idea that I'd call my oldest brother, who was working at Maryland's biggest university system at the time. My other brothers and sisters were deep into their careers, but this brother had only been working at his job for a very short period of time. I knew that getting him to work for me full time would be a long shot, but I had to try before resorting to reading all those magical résumés that can make a street walker look like the queen of England. So, I called him.

"Hey, I need to ask you something." I was really tense because all I could think about was what I would do if he said no. "What do you think about quitting your job and working for me full time?"

Without hesitation, he said, "Can you match what I'm being paid now?" He told me his salary.

"Yes!" I emphatically responded.

"Okay," he said. "When do I start?"

"Give your employer two weeks' notice and I'll see you then."

Here's my logic in response to all those who said they know too much about their family members: How much do you really know about the person who just sent you their résumé? How much can you verify in this day and age, when it is now illegal for former employers to share information with potential employers? What's the truth about the man who said that he led his department? Was he the boss or did he mean that he led his department out of the building during fire drills? When she says that she was the go-between for the president and the rank and file of the company, did she mean that she was the liaison or was she the messenger girl? You will be at a disadvantage because of how prohibitive the laws are.

Unfortunately, it could be a while before you find out the truth about your new hires. At a church I once attended, Madame Minister Meanie Mae was so evil, that I'm pretty sure that when she stirred her coffee, she stirred it hard and long and then quickly reversed the stir just to agitate it. But don't start with the ol' "That's why I don't go to church" and the ol' "See? They're as bad as I am," routine. There's much more to this. The two pastors under whom I served at that church knew that she was a Tasmanian devil with glasses. I admired both pastors deeply because of some of the advice they had given me whenever I wanted them to punch her in her rock-hard face. She was the preacher from the black lagoon!! I wasn't an official at the church at that time, so I wasn't privy to any actions that either pastor might have taken to steer her in the right direction. Neither pastor ever added fuel to the fire. So, I am making two points here. First, a minister is the last person that most folks would expect to be the troublemaker in the church. Similarly, you might never have suspected that the person in your office who is being difficult was the one who might act that way. As a business owner, what would you do with that one employee who manages to constantly disrupt the office routine? You do know that there's one in every office, don't you? With all the résumés I've reviewed, not one ever said, "Oh by the way, I'm that onion-headed troublemaker that you find in each office." The second point is that even though both pastors faced the situation at different times in their tenure, they both handled it pretty much the same way. They recognized that she was the Sinister Minister. They didn't publicly reprimand or humiliate her, and instead spoke with her privately to try to bring about a resolution. That is one excellent way to begin the resolution to that type of personnel issue. Oh sure. I say that now that I have all this business savvy. But back then? I would've fed her to the lions if I didn't think the lions would have spit her nasty butt back out! Imagine you as the manager/owner in Wicked Witch Wilhelmina's situation. As an entrepreneur, you'll find yourself smack dab in the middle of that scenario soon enough. Ready yourself!

Who Are Your Clients?

I just finished discussing how much you really know about your new employee hires. The same question applies to your clients. What do you really know about your patrons when they're outside of your office? Of course, you probably do know something about their lives, because depending on your business, they may supply a lot of personal details to you. But do you know what *kind* of people they are?

I was watching the news one night while lying in bed, and the anchorwoman, Sharon, was reporting on a murder that had occurred the night before. When she mentioned the victim's name, I sat straight up. "Whoa! I've got a client by that same name!" For

> **"What do you really know about your patrons when they're outside of your office?"**

the next several seconds, I just kept thinking that it couldn't possibly be the same person. Then they showed a picture. Wham, it hit me! If you've ever been informed of an acquaintance's murder, you know that feeling of disbelief that shoots through your head. *Oh my goodness!* I exclaimed to myself. *It really is Jed! What in the . . . Why did someone . . . Who would . . . Okay. As soon as I get in the office tomorrow, I'll get his number from the files and call his home.* The next morning came and I called immediately. His girlfriend with whom he lived, answered the phone. I could hear his mother, Gladys, who also lived there, distraught in the background.

"Hi Jenny. This is Teddy The Tax Man. I was watching the news last night, and uh, the reporter, uh . . . "

"Yes Teddy. It's true! It was Jed."

"Wow, Jenny! What happened? I'm so sorry. Have you got any answers yet?"

"No. But I'll tell you one thing. If I find the person who did it, I guarantee that you won't need to call the police on the [bad-word-here, bad-word-here, bad-word-here]! I'll take care of business myself!"

"I sure do understand that, Jenny, just be careful that you don't go overboard and end up being on the other side of the law yourself."

"Teddy, right now your advice is falling on deaf ears. This is the man that I was going to marry—spend the rest of my life with—have little babies with. What do I do now?"

In tax school, they didn't teach me expressions of condolences. They taught me what I paid them to teach me: tax preparation. And they taught me well! But this? Two weeks and a number of tax refunds later, as the shock of the incident wore off, I was in the same bed, in the same position, watching the same anchorwoman give the news.

"Police are reporting that they have made arrests in the murder of Jed Matthews."

I sat straight up. Man! I immediately thought to call Jenny or Miss Gladys, but then I realized that the police wouldn't alert the media about the arrests unless they first notified the family, so I was certain that they knew already.

"Let's go to our reporter in front of police headquarters for the latest."

"That is correct, Sharon. After days of long hard hours and plain old-fashioned detective work, police say they have made arrests in the murder of Jed Matthews. Let's hear it right from the police commissioner."

"We are pleased to announce that arrests have been made in the Jed Matthews murder. We now have in custody, Jenny Magnis, the girlfriend of Jed Matthews." Reader, as you might imagine, I was floored! It took everything I had to remain sitting up in my bed. The commissioner continued.

"We are extremely confident that we have the right individuals in custody in Miss Magnis and the second suspect, Gladys Matthews, the victim's mother."

WHAT? His own mother? What kind of stuff is this? His fiancée and his own mother? Not even his fiancée and his fiancee's mother, which would be bad enough! What kind of mental shortage could a person suffer that would cause a mother to murder her own son with the help of his girlfriend?

This incident taught me that few personal relationships are sacred nowadays. If personal relationships are tenuous, then you've got to know that there is little loyalty in business relationships, and as a business owner, you'll have to be prepared to face that fact. Take Snake for instance.

Snake had been a client of mine for about four years. He was a truck driver who was conniving (strike one), willing to do anything to get a tax refund (strike two), and a talk radio listener (strike three, four and five). Snake had referred a few clients to me over the years, and I was very thankful. One year he came in

> " you've got to know that there is little loyalty in business relationships, and as a business owner, you'll have to be prepared to face that fact. "

and sat across the desk from me as normal. But instead of pulling out his tax documents, he began to speak.

"Now Teddy, I've been coming to you for a few years now." I thought to myself, *Uh oh. Where is this appointment headed?*

"Yep, and I've always paid you your fee."

Well, shouldn't you have? I thought to myself.

"And plus, Teddy, I've even brought you a number of referrals."

"You sure have, Snake, and I've always told you that I really appreciate it."

"Well, what I want is for you to do my return for free. I think I deserve it."

"But Snake, if I start giving you discounts and free tax return preparation, I'll have to do that for everybody who brings me a referral."

"Well Teddy, I'm not talking about everybody else. I'm just talking about me."

"Snake, I'm a professional. I'm not a used car salesman."

"Well you know what, if you don't do my tax return for free after all that I've done for you, I'm walking out and going to another tax professional."

"Sorry, Snake. I can't do what you're asking me to do."

"Well then okay, Teddy. I'll see you around."

It's a good thing that I don't say everything that I'm thinking. What I actually said was, "Well, okay. I'll see you around." But what I was really thinking was, *"Alright, then. Get out! And take your sister's children that you were illegally claiming, with you!"* But I'm thick on diplomacy in my personal life. It is just as important that you, as a business owner or future owner, exercise diplomacy at the office.

> " It is just as important that you, as a business owner or future owner, exercise diplomacy at the office. "

I didn't say that diplomacy reigned supreme ALL the time! In the late 90s, a young lady came in needing her refund fast. Really fast. I don't recall whether she was delinquent on her car loan, about to get evicted or saw a pair of "must-have" blue jeans at the mall that were about to go off sale (you know, the ones I could've bought from the surplus store, put holes in them and sold to her for 1/3 of the retail price). I was offering a lightning-quick refund service back then and was ready to come to her rescue. That type of refund was normally in my office the very next day. That was during the era when the Infernal Revenue Service began ramping up their option of delaying a taxpayer's tax refund. After I prepared the return, I gave the young lady her copies along with a letter. The letter stated clear as day, that the IRS could delay any federal refund, in part or in its entirety, pending their review of the client's situation. And that was regardless of whether the return was electronically filed or not. Of her $2500, the IRS sent her about $400. When I told her this, BAM—all smell broke loose. She brought her mother and father to the office, crying and arguing that I had wronged her. While she and her father were in my face arguing, the mother headed to the waiting room where other clients were waiting. As she headed back, she hollered, "Everybody run! Run for your lives before Teddy cheats you!" I went after her and told her that if she said one more word, that I would throw her out on her bathtub-shaped butt. I don't think that sounded good to her, because she immediately stopped, came back to where we were standing and hid behind her husband. It finally hit him that his daughter could've prevented all this if she had showed him the letter that I showed him while his wife was giving her best Paul Revere imitation. I certainly could've been more diplomatic in that scenario, and it did teach me a thing or two about how one situation can paint a picture of a business to those on the outside looking in. Clients who were in the office at the time still remember the incident. Ahh yes! Physician, heal thyself!

Candee had been a client of mine for six years. She was married, relatively quiet, attractive in a black-rimmed glasses kind of way, and in her early thirties. When she came in for her appointment, things started very normally. We exchanged pleasantries, briefed each other about our families, and began. She started pulling out her statements and other necessary items for completing the tax return. I noticed three W-2 forms. One was for her, one for her husband Scott, and there was another one for someone named Bill.

"Candee, you gave me three W-2s. Who is Bill?"

"Oh. He's my boyfriend."

"Boyfriend?"

"Yeah, my boyfriend."

"Uh, I see." I really didn't see, but I had to say something.

"Yeah, Teddy. I want to see whether it would be best to file jointly with Scott or Bill."

At that point, Candee had me really lost.

"Candee, you can't file jointly unless you're married."

"I *AM* married!"

"Let me rephrase that, Candee. You can't file jointly unless you're married to the person with whom you're filing jointly."

"Are you kidding, Teddy The Tax Man? Okay. Give me back Bill's W-2. He's not going to like it. I'm gonna tell him to talk to his congressman about that!" Note: She was not blonde!

You could never meet a gentler, kinder, more personable man than Art. Art was in his early fifties, unmarried and very easy to get along with. His source of joy was an eating establishment that he had owned for some years. He came to me to help him solve a major problem. He began to explain.

"Teddy, I'm not supposed to tell you who sent me, because the person works at the Internal Revenue Service and could be fired for recommending you to me. But according to this person, if you can't help me, nobody can."

"Okay, Art. I understand. So, what can I do for you?"

"Well, a while ago, I was ready to move onto something different, so I decided to sell my restaurant. I invited a few prospective buyers in, some serious, some not, and some who just couldn't come close to my asking price. One day, I was sitting with a gentleman who was interested in purchasing the place. Things were going well. We laughed, joked and just had an overall whale of a good time. I showed him around and he seemed really pleased at what he saw. We went back to the table where we started out, nice crisp sodas awaiting our return. After a few more pleasantries, I asked him what he thought. He asked me how much money the business brought in every year, and I chuckled and told him, "Well, it depends on which of my books I show you. According to one set of books, I make this amount. But according to my real books, the ones over here, I make twice as much! And Teddy, his response gave me the shock of my life."

"'Jim Bunting. IRS!' He pulled out his badge and flashed it in my face. I wanted to crawl under the table! I mean, I could see my life flash before my eyes! Anyway, to make a long story short, I owe them $113,000. I don't have $113,000, so I want you to negotiate with the IRS, and do an offer in compromise. Can you do that for me?"

What a mess! An offer in compromise occurs when a person negotiates and reaches a settlement with the IRS to pay a smaller amount than what he/she actually owes. I'm not patting myself on the back, but I did a heck of a job negotiating with the Internal Revenue Service and Art got off by paying $13,000 and going on with his life. An excellent handling of a client's situation, if I have to say so myself. I guess I *am* patting myself on the back, and I don't care what you think about it!

But I haven't even told you about two crooks, uh, I mean clients, no, no, I meant what I said at first, CROOKS, who were clients of mine. These two birds of a feather never flocked together, but they must have learned from the same con man. One came to me already owing the Internal Revenue Service his right leg and a part of his left elbow. The other was a joker who owned a few businesses. The first one needed me to do an offer in compromise with the IRS. The second flim-flam man needed me to prepare his business's tax returns. I didn't have any pre-conceived notions about either one, but as I continued to meet with them, things started to show. You know the saying regarding peeling the onion back, and seeing more and more? I think these two were poster boys for that expression. They both were tricksters. They both were trying to beat the system (and me). They both were only concerned about the present, and they both regularly parked their cars far away from my office door, so that I wouldn't see their fancy, expensive vehicles! Yep! Can you imagine? That way, they could cry broke, and expect me to agree to a lesser fee. This dastardly duo of deceptive demons had no clue that I was onto their games. The fun in these situations is that I knew that neither one knew that I knew! If I ever see either one again, it will be too soon.

Ms. Donna and her husband Clyde were longtime clients. She called me one day to give me some news.

"Hi Teddy. My husband and I will be coming in for our appointment next week. I hit the lottery for $2500."

"Oh, you did, Ms. Donna?"

"Yep, I sure did, and I need to ask you a favor."

"Okay, what can I do for you?"

"Well, during our appointment, we will follow our normal routine. You know, he'll hand you his tax information and I'll hand you mine. Okay Teddy?"

"Sure, Ms. Donna. Why are you telling me this? We've been doing the same thing for many years."

"Well, when I hand you my statement showing the $2500 in gambling winnings, please don't read it out aloud."

"I don't understand, Ms. Donna."

"Teddy, Clyde can't read. So as long as you don't say what it is out loud, I am home free!"

I once got a phone call from a pastor who had been a client for six or seven years. A twenty-something-year-old young man (we'll call him Lucky Scott) was "headed in the wrong direction" and the pastor was hoping that I could help him with his new retail business, in which he sold clothing out of his car. I told him that sure I could. I love helping young people out anyway. He brought the young man to the office one evening and we went over the dos and don'ts of retailing, what he had to do regarding employees and payroll, filing deadlines and what to watch out for as far as running a business in general. I felt it was a good meeting. The pastor felt it was a good meeting. Lucky thought it was a good meeting. After a few additional phone calls, we were ready to finish up his tax return. I called to give him his results. "Well, you'll owe just a few hundred dollars to the IRS and a few hundred dollars to Maryland." I gave him instructions on how to pay and finished up the phone call by telling him, "My fee is four hundred dollars."

"Four hundred dollars, Teddy? Whew! Okay, let's meet at the pastor's second workplace (because despite what most people think, very few pastors are breaking the bank) and you can give me the tax forms and I'll pay you."

I thought to myself, *Hmm. That's strange. I wonder why he doesn't just come here to the office.* Anyway, a few days later, we met at the pastor's other workplace. You must picture this: We stood in the parking lot with our cars next to each other and facing opposite directions, both driver doors wide open, discussing the end results of the return. He puzzled me again when he did something else that seemed odd. He put his balled-up hand inside of mine, slowly opened it up, and out came the four hundred dollars. It was eerie. The way he looked at me didn't help. I just felt really strange all over. Anyway, as I waved to Lucky and the pastor and pulled off, the young lady whom I had brought with me just kind of looked at me. I guess I still had that "I-just-saw-a-ghost" look on my face. I explained to her how I was feeling. We talked about it for a bit while riding down I-95, but then moved on to life. Weeks later, I was watching my favorite show, the news, when a breaking story began.

Reporter: Authorities have arrested Lucky Scott for drug dealing.

Me: *What? Oh my goodness!*

That strange, weird, odd feeling just ran through my body again.

Reporter: After an extensive undercover investigation, federal marshals . . .

Me: *Federal marshals? Wait a minute! This has got to be more than just your average drug dealing on the corner, selling nickel-bags situation.*

Reporter: . . . charging Lucky Scott as a kingpin.

Me: *Oh my gosh! A kingpin? Those crazy feelings I had were legitimate. The way he handed me the money. The way he looked at me. Then I thought about times that federal marshals could've been watching ME! They could've been scoping me out in the parking lot! They could've bugged my office! They could've tapped my office phone! They could've tapped my home phone—again (but that too is another story)! They could have had me followed! They could have done surveillance on me! They could have put a tracking device on my car! They could have looked at these major muscles in my arms and thought I was an enforcer!*

Reporter: Authorities say Scott was responsible for a drug ring that generated more than forty million dollars per year in illegal drug sales.

Me: *Forty million dollars per year? Forty million dollars? And he was complaining about my four-hundred dollar fee? Just wait! I'm going to give him a piece of my mind when he gets out in the year 2098!*

Miscellaneous, Yet Not Miniscule

I've lived long enough to witness the evolution of the résumé. I think I'm going to write the editors at Merriam Webster and ask that they add the term "résumaybe" to the dictionary. Because maybe the applicant did all the things listed on the résumé, but maybe not. As I previously mentioned, there aren't many ways for you as an employer to verify those claims anymore. Back in the seventies, it was standard to provide the prospective new employer as much information as possible. In the early eighties, the wisdom was to do whatever you needed to do in order for your résumé to stand apart from the others (special fonts, using colored paper and envelopes, etc.). In the late eighties, the wisdom was to streamline your résumé because employers really didn't

have time to sort through all the Peter-Pan-type information listed, and also to make sure that you sent a thank you letter after the interview. Gag!! (Let me take my finger out of my throat. To me, that always seemed like the ultimate kiss-up). When the twenty-first century rolled around, electronic applications became the norm. "We'll only accept your résumé electronically, and résumés received by snail mail will be discarded." I predict that sometime soon, job listings will contain the following warning: "Phone calls to us regarding the status of your application could jeopardize your chances of securing this job." In fact, I recommend that you, as a prospective employer, consider using similar verbiage when you create the job listing. It's not the good ol' days anymore, and every person at the jobsite is now wearing way more hats than ever before. Who's going to have time to answer phone calls regarding whether someone's résumé, otherwise called the full-of-fallacy form, was ever received? Additionally, this could be one of the first tests in determining who can follow directions, and if a prospective employee can't follow simple instructions during this process, that might be your first clue that this individual may not be a desirable candidate to have as an actual living, breathing person in your operations.

> " if a prospective employee can't follow simple instructions during this process, that might be your first clue that this individual may not be a desirable candidate "

Somehow or another, you have made it through the resume/application process. You've laughed at the misspellings, cringed at the grammar, and were driven crazy by the run-on sentences that are still running. You've now got the next step to look forward to: the interview process. Oh joy! I can hear you jumping up and down and clicking your heels at the same time! When you are conducting your first-ever interviews as an employer, you will likely have flashbacks of the times you were invited in for a meeting with a prospective employer. You will remember tales of other interviews. I certainly remember in or around 1984 when my boss was interviewing Bo, a prospect for a computer operator's job. The interview was going pretty well for the first half-hour or so, until my boss asked about the types of computers Bo had operated previously.

"So, Bo, in your last job, what was the process for starting up the computer?"

"Well, I always had to make sure the hard drives were ready to be powered up, the tape drives were set and then hit the power button and listen for all the peripheral equipment to rev up."

"Oh. I see. That's very similar to our operation. Did you also use IBM?"

"Yes. We did."

"What was the process for re-IPL'ing (rebooting) the system?"

To my boss's surprise, Bo blurted out, "Darn!" (I'm being nice. He didn't quite use the term "darn.") "What do you want me to do? Make the computer?"

Now, nothing can stop me from buying Bo's book on how to win the job during the interview!

I once interviewed a young lady who made an embarrassing error. We had gotten off the subject of skills, duties and responsibilities and had started to talk about how colds, flu and other sicknesses wreak havoc in the workplace.

"Natalie, I really need to let you know that one of my greatest concerns is that I don't want to hire anybody who is consistently absent. It makes things extremely difficult on everyone else in the office, especially in a very small office."

"Oh, but you don't have to worry about me, Mr. Teddy the Taxman! I'm a health freak and most of the vitamins that I take have euthanasia in them."

Now, I'm certain that she meant "echinacea." Either that, or it's impossible for that lady to die. This mistake made her seem unintelligent, or perhaps uneducated. But then again, maybe this interviewee was just nervous. I know that I get very nervous around some people and I can't seem to manage to express myself properly. I may as well fill a balloon with water and tie it to my tongue when I talk! Yet, I can speak to one million television viewers per year without a teleprompter or script, and be as smooth as silk. What I'm saying is, how much can a prospective employer get out of a one-hour meeting with a prospective employee?

Also remember that humans (except for Bo, our computer operator extraordinaire wannabe) tend to show their best sides when they think it's necessary. After the interview, however, they revert to cursing out the nun who bumped into them in the hallway. There is a parallel here to the dating or courting process. When a guy takes a girl to the all-you-can-eatery on a date, she offers to fix your plate. Now once she's his wife, the phrase "every man for himself" is her credo. So, beware—no one ever promised you a rose garden. The interview process is tough, no matter how you look at it, and sometimes you have to follow your instincts.

> **"The interview process is tough, no matter how you look at it, and sometimes you have to follow your instincts."**

My daughter Renatta, born in the late eighties, worked for me for a while. She would often ask me, "Oh my goodness, Daddy! Why are you wearing *that* with *that*?" Yeah, right! Like I'm going to take fashion advice from a generation that believes belt loops are an accessory. Besides, this is the same daughter who walked out of the office, started her car, came back in the office and let it run, gas a-burning while she worked for half an hour, and when I asked her why, she responded, "When I mistakenly leave my wall charger home, that's how I charge my cell phone!" Bone of my bone? Flesh of my flesh? Whew!

But the very first time I took her to one of my meetings where I brainstormed with other investment professionals, she blew them away with suggestions and comments that we, the older generation, would have never considered. Point? It taught me to appreciate the perspective of another generation in my office, and that if one of my objectives was to draw that generation in as part of my clientele, it would probably behoove me to open up just a little to an employee in that same age range. I mean, I didn't get ridiculous with it and go out to get an earring in my navel, but I did become enlightened.

Like me, you may be very surprised at the number of high level folks who lack some of the most basic skills. And you'll certainly wonder how they got where they are. I remember that during my first computer job, there was a gentleman, Fred, who couldn't spell a lick . . . and probably couldn't even spell l-i-c-k. But I guarantee you that every time our computer system went down, the computer system on which tens of thousands of banking customers and ATMs depended, he was able to figure out the issue and bring it back up. That situation and a slew of others over these many years showed me something very important that I want you to consider. That is, in a blue-collar environment, don't expect Aristotle or Maya Angelou. Don't expect your construction worker, home improvement professional or auto mechanic to win a spell-a-thon. It won't happen. This will be one of the times that you'll have to put behind you all that you ever learned regarding what to look for in a résumé. I'm not suggesting that you excuse the 10W40 oil that's smeared all over the résumé. I'm saying, be careful where you draw the line.

> " you may be very surprised at the number of high level folks who lack some of the most basic skills. "

If you happen to be starting a tax practice, make sure that all your fees are spelled out clearly. This is how I'm considering doing mine from now on:

Personal Tax Preparation: $350
Business Tax Preparation: $1,100
Representation: $1,000
Referee Fee: $5,000

Oh yes! You *will* need to implement the referee fee! I know you've heard of divorcing couples fighting over the house, or fighting over the money, or the children, or even the pets! The breaker for me was the divorcing couple fighting over the bonus number that allowed them to get a discount at their supermarket! I'M DONE!

I was leaving the office one day during the tax rush, just short of 9:30 PM. I was tired, hungry and thirsty. I was dragging. I had about thirty-to-forty yards to go before I could sink into my car and just get comfortable for my ride home. As I passed dark office after empty dark office, I noticed that one business's light was on. It's probable that even if the blinds were completely closed, I would've still noticed the shadowy movement of the person who obviously was as dedicated a worker as I was, to be working so far into the night. With a smile on my face, and ready to make some smart aleck remark, like "I-get-to-go home-and-you-don't," I balled up my fist, prepared to give a quick knock to gain the person's attention. Then I stopped my fist in mid-air. Either that one person I saw through the blinds had four legs, or it was two people that I was seeing. And since I've never seen a four-legged human wear a pair of pants on two legs and a dress on the other two at the same time, I knew that I was mistaken. Boy was I mistaken! And I'm certain that work was the farthest topic from their minds. Yep. Man and woman, in relative solitude, with no pens and no pads. They were kissing and hugging like there was no tomorrow. I couldn't hear what they were whispering, but I let my vivid imagination (that my eighth grade English teacher just could not quite grasp) run wild. They dropped straight down behind the desk together, still lip-locked, and shedding those pesky clothes as they went. I immediately reached into my pocket and pulled out my cell phone. I simply had to call one of my best buddies and give a play-by-play on the action. I began dialing his 10 digits. Digit number 1. Digit number 2. Digit number 3. Digit number 4. [Loud male voice inside, screaming and interrupting the peace of the night]. Digit number 5. Digit number 6. Digit number 7. Digit number 8 . . . *Wait a minute! He's standing back up? He's zipping up? Can't be!! Can it?* Yep. The look on her face as she lay there told me everything. If this were a cartoon in the newspaper, you'd see the big bubble over her head with the words, "You mean I missed scraping gook off of dirty dishes in the sink at home for this?" I'll go out on a limb and say that she's still telling that story to her girlfriends today!

Then there is the story about the oh-so-proud mother executive. She had two young sons. One was seven, and one was five. She and I were meeting with an IRS officer at my place of business. Fortunately, it was a situation that was working in my client's favor, so there wasn't any angst or nervousness. The five-year-old called the office to speak to his mother. Mama was beaming because the five-year-old was getting to be as self-sufficient as any other five-year-old, and she wanted the IRS officer and me to know it, so she put her son on speaker phone.

"Mom, didn't you tell me that whenever I go to the bathroom, I have to wash my hands when I finish?"

Mom, looking quite pleased said, "Yes dear, I did."

"So, if I don't go, do I still have to wash?"

Mom, looking a little puzzled, said, "Of course not."

We could hear the seven-year-old's voice in the background, obviously trying to convey a message to Mom via the long-distance-hollering method, and we could tell that the five-year old had turned away from the phone to holler to the seven-year-old.

"See? Mom said that I don't have to wash my hands if I just reach in to scratch for a few minutes!"

My client Sandy had a boyfriend named Barney who intentionally gave the wrong social security number to a business for which he was doing some subcontracting work. That meant that, whatever income he earned, no taxes would be withheld.

So, for at least twelve years, he laughed at the system because he wasn't paying taxes. I haven't seen Barney since probably around 2004, but one time before then when he came in with Sandy for his appointment, he jokingly reminded me that he still wasn't paying taxes. I finally said to him, "What are you going to do when you retire and there's no social security or company 401(k) waiting for you?" He looked at Sandy, smiled and nodded in her direction.

> " You haven't made it as a business if you've never been sued! "

"She's going to take care of me." I can't print Sandy's comeback here, but trust me, she vehemently disagreed with his ill-conceived plan. I can guarantee you that when the time comes, he'll apply for some type of public assistance and get it, after years of not paying into the system. Reader, are you angry yet?

If the Suit Fits . . .

You haven't made it as a business if you've never been sued! So please announce to the public that I have made it! Yep. I got sued. Over the course of thirty years and more than 15,000 tax returns, I had never been dragged into a courthouse, until some joker decided that he wanted what I had. Didn't he know that I hate court?

Speaking of court, I always forget that being a plaintiff or defendant in court has nothing to do with truth. But I was reminded pretty fast and pretty thoroughly when I told a client that I had to go to court for a personal issue. Alright, alright! It was my divorce!! He said, "Oh Teddy! They're going to shred you!!" I told him that I didn't think so, because I had all the data that I needed to prove that they shouldn't shred me. He looked at me as if to say, "You fool! Don't you know that this is America? It doesn't work that way!" What he actually said was, "Believe me. It makes no difference. They'll take practically everything that you have. Believe me. I've been there and done that. And I've witnessed it many times." I started to believe him. He had no reason to mislead me. But this is what took it over the top for me: the judge that was assigned to my case was the same Maryland judge who was eaten alive by women's groups all over the country, when he stupidly insinuated during a trial that he had overseen, that a defendant's rape of an inebriated young lady amounted to nothing. WHAT? The following is an excerpt of the horrible and insensitive thought process of a nutcase in a black robe, as printed by *The Baltimore Sun* on October 28, 1994:

> . . . their signs also referred to Judge Thomas J. Bollinger, whose offer of probation before judgment and sympathetic comments in sentencing a 44-year-old man convicted of raping a drunken 18-year-old woman, provoked similar outcries last year.

Can you believe that? Well I knew what I had to do then. I did it, and that's all you need to know!

Regrets

f I'm ever asked that certain question that is inevitably asked of folks who contribute to society, and I answer no, don't believe me. I beg you. Don't believe me! That's right. Please! It cracks me up when I watch an interview and the host asks the guest the question: "Do you have any regrets?" I've never, ever heard anyone say yes. They always say that they have none. SHAAAADAAAAAAAAP!

I'd like to think that I did everything perfectly in my years as a tax professional. Think about it: in second grade, a perfect score on a test grandfathered you in as teacher's pet. But I know that I didn't always do everything perfectly. I still have second thoughts about some of the decisions I made in life and specifically in my practice. I still regret that in 1976 when my driving instructor asked if I wanted to learn to drive a stick shift or an automatic, I told him that I wanted to learn the automatic. Today, I still have no clue as to how to drive a stick shift. In my practice? Well, one day in the early nineties, a new client came in. She was middle-aged, unmarried, unemployed and like everybody else, hoping for a refund. I had to be the bearer of bad news. There was no refund forthcoming. In fact, she was going to owe the IRS quite a bit.

> " I didn't always do everything perfectly. I still have second thoughts about some of the decisions I made in life and specifically in my practice. "

"What would my end result be if I didn't report the unemployment income on my tax return?" she asked. I told her that that was a moot point because she's required by law to report unemployment. "I know, I know, Teddy, but I'm just dying to know. It's eating at me!"

"Okay, Ms. Lisa. Let's see. Well, you would've gotten a nice refund."

"Well, can we just not report the unemployment?"

"I'm sorry, but we can't do that."

"But you don't understand, Teddy. I really need money."

"Yeah, I do understand, and it's not that I don't empathize with you, but I just can't participate in that kind of thing," I explained.

She cried a little and whimpered and whined even more. After several minutes, she propositioned me. "I'll tell you what. What if I gave you one hundred extra dollars to take out the unemployment income?"

"Huh? One hundred extra dollars? You mean you'll give me $100 on top of my fee if we took out the unemployment income?"

"Yeah, Teddy. I really need that refund. I'm desperate! I'm behind on my rent, my car is going to be repossessed, and I don't know what I'll do if I don't get money soon."

I thought about it for less than a minute, then agreed to take the unemployment off the tax return. She ended up with a nice refund and I ended up with an extra $100. I sold my morals. I knew it was wrong, but I let her feelings and my greed supersede the need to do right. Whatever you do, don't risk what you have for the quick buck. The guilt that you'll endure is just not worth it, and you won't even remember where the $100 went!

In 1993, a husband and his wife came to me as new clients. They were both musicians with the Baltimore Symphony Orchestra. I prepared their return and got them a nice refund and they were very satisfied. Much later, I was going through the files and noticed something. I had missed one of their W-2s, and that's how they had gotten such a good refund. How did I miss a W-2? Well, since they both worked for the same employer, their W-2s looked alike (I'm sure that you're saying, "Duh," but I hate that expression) and I thought that I was simply looking at a copy of the first one, so I disregarded it. Later, they received a nasty-gram from the IRS that said they owed about $1300. They called me and asked why. Embarrassment didn't allow me to open up and admit to them that I had made a mistake.

It's a given. Mistakes will happen in your business. How you address the mistakes can and will separate you from the rest. Here it is, years later, and those mishandled situations are still fresh in my mind, and there's nothing I can do to rid myself of those thoughts.

I regret that as a third-grader, I joined in with the others who teased a female classmate who had Tourette syndrome. I hadn't a clue as to what Tourette syndrome was. I kept telling her that she was faking, and that all that jerk-ing was unnecessary. Man, do I feel bad now! So incredibly bad, that about forty years later, I saw her for the first time since elementary school, walking in downtown Baltimore and I just had to apologize. I know that had nothing to do with owning a business, but I had to get it off my chest. No regrets? You've got to be kidding!

> " Mistakes will happen in your business. How you address the mistakes can and will separate you from the rest. "

A mentor. Get one right away! I regret not having a mentor. I never, ever even considered it. If it had come across my mind, especially in the very early days, I would've begged someone to lead me through the underbelly of the income tax world. I can only imagine where I'd be right now. I mean having access to someone who has been in practice for a number of years longer than me . . . someone who I could bounce ideas off of . . . I realize now that would have saved me a lot of time and from making a lot of mistakes and learning the hard way. If you are headed to the world of "pay-yourself," I highly recommend making that move. You could try to scope out that knowledgeable person in your group, your club, your professional organization, etc., and go through the back door to sidle up to that person and start to get acquainted. Maybe you will hit it off and it could be the start of a beautiful mentoring relationship, and you can start your sponging. The other option is for you to pay someone a small stipend to be at the ready, so that when you needed to reach out, you could do just that. That's not the typical way to go about it, and as an entrepreneur, you'll certainly have more than your fair share of expenses already, but if you set it up that way, you are certainly more likely to have a greater access to answers that could change your direction in a very positive way.

Although I never had a mentor, I did come close. Twice. The very first time that I wanted to try tax software, I called a company called Drake. It was 1990, and Drake was at the top of the leaderboard when it came to this brand new movement called electronic filing. Later, Drake software became *the* tax software to use, when many commercial tax preparation software companies began to go the way of the mailed paper tax return, meaning that they disappeared off the face of the earth. I even found out that the Internal Revenue Service itself was using it at the time, for its own purposes. What? The IRS using professional commercial tax preparation software? I had never tried any other company, and didn't want to spend weeks upon weeks testing, searching and re-searching, so Drake asked Thel Moore, Sr., owner of Moore's Tax Service in Baltimore, if he didn't mind allowing me to come in and disrupt his office, to put the software to the test. He could've very easily said no, but he didn't. He welcomed me in and gave me as much time as I needed. He even raved about the tax prepa-ration software. Well, I had never used computer-based software at all, whereas this was probably Thel's third season. Was I going to disregard a recommendation from a person in that position? Well, because of that one meeting, we became friends and col-leagues for the next twenty-seven years and beyond. And get this: Back in 1990, he told me that after looking at how the other software vendors operated, Drake Software seemed as if it could be around for years and years to come. I am clueless as to what he saw in that company, but he was on the money! Through 2017, I have no idea how many hundreds of thousands of professional tax preparers use that particular commercial software, but I can probably name twenty-something software companies that have

> " having access to someone who has been in practice for a number of years longer than me . . . someone who I could bounce ideas off of . . . I realize now that would have saved me a lot of time and from making a lot of mistakes and learning the hard way. "

disappeared. That's the kind of advice that I'd seek from a mentor!

The second time that I blew an opportunity at obtaining a mentor, well, let's just say that I could've kicked myself! I was thirteen years into my tax preparation career, and up to that point, I had been very intent on preparing tax returns for individual taxpayers. I decided that it was time to expand into the business tax preparation realm. The tax preparation landscape had begun to change, and the number of fraudulent returns prepared for individuals really soared off the charts. (And it's funny how the IRS thinks that less than thirty percent of all taxpayers cheat on their taxes. Pshaw! Make that about ninety-two percent of people who itemize!) Well, a tax professional can't venture into preparing returns for C-corporations, LLC's, non-profits and other business entities without knowing accounting.

It's impossible. I enrolled in Accounting I, at Essex Community College in Maryland. After the first few days, I honestly could not understand why so many people hated accounting. I couldn't! Mr. Michael Ryan could probably teach the Atlantic Ocean not to wave! I mean, he made it that easy! The only way he could've made it easier for us would have been if he had given us the answers. Honestly, that would've been okay with me! But if you've ever been in a position in which things were going so well that you could not believe it, and you found yourself waiting for the other shoe to drop, you know exactly what I mean. This instructor had a method of teaching that even I could understand. I found myself attending all of his accounting I classes. If I was in his 10:00 AM class, and he had a 12:30 class, I would take the morning class, go home, and be back in time for the 12:30 class. After a few weeks, he noticed what I was doing, and jokingly called me out in front of the class. I learned from him what I set out to learn, and I'll bet that had I asked him to mentor me, he would have. I didn't, and ouch! I can feel it now. I'm going to kick myself after this sentence.

No regrets? Hmph! I was a serious baseball fan as a youngster in the sixties. I absolutely loved the game. I played in the little leagues. I played the "broken-glass alley" circuit. I loved the Baltimore Orioles like crazy! One day, we went to the game. I was in my normal "love Frank-Paul-Brooks-Boog" euphoric state, and I was really enjoying the game. Big time! My seat was near first base and was the closest I had ever been to the field in my young innocent life. I could have brought my clothes to the stadium and moved permanently into that seat if a television had been attached to it. The game was moving along. Then, a controversial call was made on a very close play. My favorite player rushed up and started yelling and screaming at the umpire. From where I was sitting, I could hear practically everything! I could only think that if my favorite player was arguing, he must have been right. And then it happened. In the midst of the hollering, I heard it. I heard my favorite player curse! *Did he really say that?* I thought to myself. *Did he really use that word? Wow! I didn't know base-ball players said curse words!* I'm certain that my eyes were as wide as fifty-cent pieces. I felt so dejected, I don't even remember who won the game. I think for probably the next few weeks, that revelation was very heavy on my mind. I don't think I ever told anyone about that incident and how it impacted me. What does that have to do with running a business? Well, just wait until that great big revelation unfolds regarding that employee who you never thought would've ever done something like what you just found out was done. But it's important to stay focused. Was the deed illegal? Was it at the job? Was it in the office? How much will it affect the rest of the employees? Is it fair to fire said employee? If you don't, what message does that send to the others? Regrets?

" **it's important to stay focused.** "

I don't have any idiosyncrasies. I mean, I'm sure that I'm not the only one who, when he's on his way out the house and on his way to a fast food restaurant, washes his hands, drives all the way to the restaurant with his left hand closed and touching nothing (to be used as the primary eating hand), just so that he doesn't have to go into a nasty bathroom to wash them again, and spoil his appetite so much that he can't eat in the first place. There's no way that I can be the only one.

You will regret your idiosyncrasies getting in the way of your business dealings and/or your employee-to-boss communications.

> " You will regret your idiosyncrasies getting in the way of your business dealings and/or your employee-to-boss communications. "

I've never been a sore loser. Nope. Never! Not even when I was in the sixth grade and lost the election for student government president to Karen M. Nope. Not even then. She was a virtual unknown who didn't deserve to win, because I was smarter than she was. Everybody loved me, not her. Everybody respected me, not her. My grades were better, I dressed better, my hair was always combed, I was a class leader, within the top class in the school, and I had more brothers and sisters than she had, and I didn't get much help in my campaign from my darned teacher like she did, plus I had been going to Fort Worthington

School #85 longer than she had, and she had the nerve to disrespect me by beating the boy who was among the top four fastest runners in the school. Who did she think she was?! But I'm not mad because I'm not a sore loser.

A Few Secrets from My Profession

Every profession I know has secrets. Here are some regarding mine:

A) Tax professionals hate you when you come in and say, "Hey! I started a business last year!"

B) By far, most men who come in and say that they are caring for their child, and it's just the two of them living in that house, are lying.

C) If you had no major changes in your situation, and all of a sudden your tax preparer doubles your fee from last year, your preparer has charged you a P-I-T-A fee, and is trying to get rid of you. And oh, by the way, you are the topic of conversation at our next conference. You do know what P-I-T-A stands for, don't you?

D) We want to throw you out the window, one limb at a time, when you complain and say that your co-worker makes the same amount of money as you did, yet he's getting more of a refund than you.

E) Ladies, when you come in and proclaim that you are divorced, and your child and you are no longer living with your husband (so that you can get a bigger refund) could you at least humor us and take the big rock off your finger before you enter the office?

Listen! Get yourself in a good position to earn a very good living. Love what you do! Don't like what you do currently as an employee? Quit and start your own! . . .

About the Author

Teddy Prioleau—widely known as Teddy The Tax Man™—is an Enrolled Agent who began his practice in 1980 and has successfully run the business since. He has been an invited guest on Fox 45 Morning News in Maryland, on which he has educated millions of viewers about retirement and tax issues that affect their families, and can be heard every Saturday morning on *Let's Get It On*, a radio program for the National Alliance of Postal and Federal Employees, where he discusses topics such as rolling over retirements, taxes, small business issues, and other financial information that is important to households at all levels of the income spectrum. Teddy is also interviewed on a regular basis on the historic Howard University Radio (WHUR.com) and many other radio stations around the country. He is the past chairman-of-the-board of a 12,000-member credit union, past vice-chairman of The Maryland Tax Preparers board, and past chairman of the membership committee of the Maryland Society of Accountants, and continues to serve on other boards that gladly use his talents to further their advancement in their areas of service.

Teddy The Tax Man™ recently celebrated the preparation of his 20,000th tax return. Twenty-thousandth!!! In 2010, Teddy expanded his retirements practice to prepare for the onslaught of those who are leaving their jobs for retirement or are headed towards a second career. He is the founder of Hunt Valley Retirements, LLC, in the beautiful town of Hunt Valley, Maryland. One of the many, many highlights of his life was appearing on *Family Feud* on November 9th, 2017, with four of his siblings.

Hunt Valley Retirements, LLC

*Rollovers, *IRAs, Life Insurance, Retirements, Notary Services

Teddy Prioleau*

Teddy@HuntValleyRetirements.com

9 Schilling Rd Suite 104
Hunt Valley, MD 21031

Phone: 410-931-2004
Fax: 1-877-232-6577

www.HuntValleyRetirements.com

*Securities offered through HD Vest Investment Services^{SM}, member SIPC

9 Schilling Rd Suite 104, Hunt Valley, MD 21031
CA Insurance Lic #0G93604
Hunt Valley Retirements, LLC is not a registered broker/dealer
or registered investment advisory firm.